HOW MUCH FAITH DOES IT TAKE ?

HOW MUCH FAITH DOES IT TAKE?

Arnold Prater

Thomas Nelson Publishers
Nashville

Published in Nashville, Tennessee, by Thomas Nelson, Inc., Publishers and distributed in Canada by Lawson Falle, Ltd., Cambridge, Ontario.

Printed in the United States of America.

Unless otherwise indicated, all Scripture verses are taken from the Revised Standard Version of the Bible, copyrighted 1946, 1952, © 1971, 1973.

Verses marked KJV are from the King James Version of the Bible.

Library of Congress Cataloging in Publication Data

Prater, Arnold.
   How much faith does it take?

   Bibliography: p.
   1. Faith—Popular works.   I. Title.
BT771.2.P64   234'.2   81-18689
ISBN 0-8407-5793-X   AACR2

This is for Louise Schermerhorn,
who claimed all the promises
but found final peace in
trusting the Promiser.

Contents

Acknowledgements

I would like to express gratitude to Margie Swift, my faithful typist who has done many manuscripts for me, including this one, and whose work always delights editors' eyes. Moreover, she is a beautiful friend in Christ.

"Miss Martha," my wife of many (I shouldn't mention how many) years, faithfully and critically listens to me read every word I have written each day, and offers all her suggestions in the spirit of love and helpfulness.

Finally, I wish to acknowledge all of the hundreds of prayers from the spiritual family of Arnold Prater Ministries, who lift us to God daily. Without those people there could be no ministry of writing.

HOW
MUCH
FAITH
DOES IT
TAKE
?

I
Will Faith
Make Me Well?

In Arkansas, not too far from where my wife and I live, there is a very humble and sincere minister whose mother died. He announced that, since Jesus had instructed his followers to "heal the sick, raise the dead, cleanse the lepers, [and] cast out demons" (Matt. 10:8), he and some of his congregation would maintain a prayer vigil by the body until she was brought back to life.

And why not, he reasoned? The instruction to raise the dead was just as specific as that to heal the sick. He had for years been conducting services of healing in his church and had seen many answers to prayer, some of them spectacular.

The vigil began in the local funeral home, and they prayed around the clock, day in and day out. After several days the local health authorities obtained a court injunction instructing the son to bury his mother's body at once.

But his faith was immovable. He found a funeral home across the state line in Missouri where laws about that sort of thing are not so strict and, after freezing the body, continued the vigil. After many, many days, they gave up and interred the remains.

What went wrong? I am sure that the minister and his followers were baffled. Because of widespread publicity, the incident caused quite a stir in the Midwest. Some people shrugged the whole thing off by labeling the group as "fanatics." Some liberal Christians said they were using the Scripture out of context. By "healing the sick [and] raising the dead," they said, Jesus had meant those who were sick in spirit and those whose hearts were dead toward God.

But such answers do not fully satisfy those who take the Word of God seriously. Furthermore, the only people who do not believe in miracle healings are those who have never experienced one.

What would have happened if the minister and his congregation had had more faith? Was lack of faith the problem? How much faith does it take to evoke a response from God?

Cheryl Prewitt, Miss America of 1980, was a personal friend of ours several years before she became famous at Atlantic City. Most of Christian America by now has either read or heard her thrilling testimony: how she was involved in a terrible auto crash at age eleven and miraculously escaped death, but she was left with one leg almost two inches shorter than the other. We heard and read her exciting story of how, with the help of the Holy Spirit, she was brought to believe that God could heal her shortened leg. Then, on one incredible night when the power of God came down, her shortened leg was made whole again.

This young woman possesses remarkable faith, sincerity, and, above all, honesty. She did not embellish her testimony to make it more interesting; she simply told it like it was. Many acquaintances who knew her before and after the miracle reiterated her account.

Marvelous, super, fantastic!

We have another dear friend who is so filled with God that his friendly round face beams like some delighted star. Lonnie Wood is a double amputee. If anyone is Spirit-filled and faith-filled, he is. Why doesn't God regenerate his legs? Is God able to heal a two-inch deficiency but stymied by an additional eighteen inches or so? Does Cheryl have more faith than Lonnie? If you knew Lonnie, you would never say that!

How much faith does it take? In some cases Jesus seemed to place a great premium on faith. Once when he approached two blind men (see Matt. 9:27–31), they cried out for healing. Jesus asked them directly, "Do you believe that I am able to do this?" They answered, "Yes, Lord." He touched their eyes and said, "According to your faith be it done to you." And their sight returned.

Is healing simply a matter of believing that He can do it? Cheryl believed God could do it, and you can be sure Lonnie believes God can do it. You may say, "Yes, but Cheryl believed that God *would* do it and perhaps Lonnie doesn't have enough faith to believe that in his own case." If you say that, you are saying faith is *quantitative*, right? Where are the dividing lines between enough, not enough, and not quite enough?

At this point we must stop to lay down the basic principles for everything I am going to say in this book. You should place it squarely in the awareness center of your mind, so that it will constantly be before you. Otherwise it is going to be impossible for us to communicate.

What you believe about faith tells me the kind of God in whom you believe. The same thing is true about prayer (I have dealt with that subject in another book[1]). You cannot escape it: The kind of God on whom you have risked everything comes shining through when you tell me what you believe about faith.

If you believe in a God who answers prayer only according to the *amount* of faith a person has, you have to deal with my question: How much faith does it take? Does it take a pound? A gallon? An ounce?

What do you do with a God who says through His Son Jesus Christ that huge amounts of faith bring miracles, as in the example of the centurion whose servant was desperately ill? He told Jesus it wasn't necessary for Him to come to his home, but if He would only speak the words a miracle was bound to happen.

Jesus heard this and was greatly impressed; in fact the Bible says, ". . . he marveled, and said to those who followed him, '. . . not even in Israel have I found such faith'" (Matt. 8:10). Then He healed the servant long distance.

This same God, our Lord Jesus Christ, said that if you have faith the size of a mustard seed, you could move mountains. I persist in asking, How much faith does it take to evoke a response from God? This comparison seems to suggest that sometimes it takes a lot and sometimes not very much. Does this mean that God is whimsical, moody, or capricious? Well, certainly none of us believe that, so there must be a better explanation.

May I pause to say that I am not an "answer man" who has come to give you a new set of religious slogans. What I offer you are concepts which have been derived from my careful searching of the Scriptures and from my own experience with God. I learned a long time ago that, if I share things which have proved biblically helpful and satisfying to me, inevitably someone else is going to be helped. That is my sole purpose for writing this book.

I do not intend to "put down" those who handle the Scriptures differently than I. Presumably, we are all on the same team, the team which aims to exalt Jesus Christ. Therefore, if they win, I win; if they lose, I lose. I am not embittered toward others who offer radically different approaches.

To those faithful who have been disappointed or hurt, to those who wish to go deeper into the roots of the "faith controversy," I want to issue a special invitation to come along with me on a thrilling and exciting journey. Let's put our hesitancy aside and plunge into this huge mystery, secure in the knowledge that we don't always have to be perfect to be saved. We need only to be His!

Once more: What you believe about faith reveals the kind of God in whom you believe. I don't believe in the kind of God who always answers our prayers or meets our needs according to our faith. Nor do I believe in a God who *only* answers prayer according to our faith. I believe in the kind of a God who often *chooses* by His mercy to pour out His power when He sees our faith, and miracles result.

When God created us with free choice He placed some voluntary restrictions upon Himself. He could not violate our choices; otherwise they would not be made in freedom. For example, God can create a rainbow and the rainbow has no choice in the matter. It cannot say to God, "I forbid you to create me." But a person can say, "I forbid you to save my soul through Jesus Christ," and God accepts the limitations He has placed upon Himself.

Sometimes God elects, in response to great faith and earnest prayer, to do what He would not do otherwise. Was this not true, for example, in the case of the penitent thief (see Luke 23:39–43) or the inopportune judge (see Luke 18:2–8)?

Sometimes miracles occur when faith does not exist at all. Read the account of the man in the synagogue with the withered hand (see Matt. 12:9–13). Here is the case of a man with an obvious need. We are not told if he had any faith in Jesus, or even if he had ever heard of Him. The man's faith is not mentioned at all. According to Matthew's account, the man never *asked* to be healed. Jesus acted out of his deeply compassionate heart in a situation wherein His heavenly Father could be glorified. He simply healed the man.

The New Testament record shows that sometimes God waits to act until He sees our faith, and sometimes He acts where we can observe no faith at all.

Who finally determines when God shall act and when He shall not? Who knows when He acts in a totally sovereign manner and when He is bound by His voluntary limitations? Who knows which answer is best in each situation? Who knows exactly what God ought to do at all times and in all situations and under all circumstances? The answer here is very simple—He does.

That is about the only answer in this controversy that is simple, for after that we run into all kinds of mysteries. For example, what about the seemingly specific promises in the Scriptures? "Truly, truly, I say to you, if you ask anything of the Father, he will give it to you in my name" (John 16:23).

Is the Word of God to be trusted? Then why is it we ask things in the name of Jesus and we do not receive them? Does faith enter into this?

We shall deal with this mystery head-on a bit further along. For now I am only making the point that God is God. He is not our lackey; He is our heavenly Father. We are never going to squeeze Him into a formula to write on heaven's blackboard and apply it when the baby is sick or Uncle John is found to have leukemia.

What a mess we would soon make of things if God placed all His awesome power at our indiscriminate disposal through a system that states that, if we do A, B, and C, God will perform miracles on demand. I want to pause and praise His name for His being wiser than that. If it were true that we could box God into a corner, potential tragedies would be happening all the time.

Writing in *The Upper Room*,[2] Carol Zebb told of a Christian sister named Dana who was awaiting the birth of her first child. The due date came and went. Three weeks passed. (Those of you who have had that experience know how miserable life can be at that particular time.) The doctor told her the heartbeat of the child was strong and everything was all right, but the child had not dropped into position for the journey through the birth canal.

"Lord, let the baby drop," Dana prayed over and over throughout the following week. At this point, had Dana been my wife, I probably would have made phone calls, written letters, and sent telegrams to enlist all the prayer power possible. I probably would have called my sharing group in, and we would have laid our hands on her and reminded God of His specific promises about asking with faith. We might even have had a prayer vigil, storming the gates of heaven, beseeching God to let the baby drop, be born, relieve Dana, and calm everyone's anxieties.

Finally, the doctor decided to deliver by Caesarean section. They found the baby's umbilical cord twisted around his neck. If he had lowered into position, he would have strangled!

There was no way anyone could have known about that. X-rays would not have revealed it. Only God knew. He answered all their prayers with the best possible answer under the circumstances.

That's the kind of God in whom I believe. How about you? That's the kind of God in whom Paul believed also, for he wrote, "We know that in everything God works for good with those who love him . . ." (Rom. 8:28). My entire life is nailed down at all four corners on that verse.

How much faith does it take? If faith is quantitative at all, it takes far less faith to fit God into a formula than it does to trust Him in the blackest midnight, when there appears to be no answer at all!

Jan McCray is a dear, vibrant Christian friend. Once she said something that pierced my soul to where it matters most. "What takes real faith," she told me, "is to trust Jesus to hear *past* what you think is best. To say, 'Lord, this is what I think my need is, but I pray you will meet my *real* need in case I'm mistaken.' "

The problem with formulas is that in practice we soon grow to trust *them*. And the formula—not the Father—becomes our Sovereign. We come to trust the promise and forget the Promiser. We make our faith the central object instead of Christ. All of this is so subtle that the Bible calls it "deception."

Since we're discussing babies and formula, let's carry the figure a bit further. A mother buys baby formula at the grocery store. She knows the brand is trustworthy. Many people have used it before. She follows the directions in detail. The nourishment works. The baby grows and suffers no ill effects. She trusts the formula. But here is where she is wrong. She should really trust the manufacturer. Certainly she does not understand all the chemical terms that are used on the label, but she does trust that the label is true and that the manufacturer has introduced no foreign or harmful matter. The label is no better than the one who made it.

Even though God's promises are trustworthy, we can risk everything on them because of who the Promiser is. God is not a colossal computer somewhere who rolls out a gigantic printout sheet with the exact answers we want, provided we have tapped the right keys.

Suppose you are a little child standing in front of a gumball machine. It is filled to the top with gum. There are at least a dozen different colors. You have what it takes to operate the machine (a dime—or is it a quarter now?) and you want a red ball of gum. You trustingly place the coin in the slot and pull the lever. You get your gum but instead of a red ball, you get a green one. How come? You did everything right. You had enough money. You believed, but the machine let you down. Because you're a little child you can't understand. You get angry at the machine. Perhaps you shake it violently, kick it, and speak harsh words to it. Finally you walk away, in tears, and declare inwardly that that's the last time you'll trust a gumball machine.

In a sense, some people believe in a gumball machine God. Although the machine is filled with many different answers, they believe if they have the correct amount of faith and pull the proper prayer lever the answer they want will *always* come rolling out.

The illustration breaks down at this point, as all illustrations depicting God ultimately must. In real life the gumball machine is mindless and impersonal. It has no feelings whatsoever toward you. You got the green gumball instead of the red not because the machine had your welfare at heart but because of blind chance.

How much faith does it take to evoke the response you desire from God? You see, the problem with quantitative faith is that it always places the monkey on our backs. We must finally determine the answers or lack of answers by the amount of faith we have.

That's too much responsibility. No father would send a weak child, immature and undeveloped, out into a world to fend for himself. No father would expect that child to know what is best for him, to know the future, or to make all the right choices so that a full and abundant life would result. A wise and loving father delegates responsibility only as the child becomes capable of assuming it.

Our heavenly Father expects faith. Indeed, He demands it. He knows it is the only way we will grow. If we have no faith, we cannot please Him nor in some cases can He grant us what He would like. He loves us too much to expect us to carry the whole load by ourselves. That is why He shares in our growth responsibilities. His love for us is the reason He took the monkey off our back and placed it on His. No, on second thought, it wasn't a monkey.

It was a cross.

II

Will Faith
Do It Now?

God sometimes answers promptly, sometimes after a long period of time. To think faith must produce immediate results each time is like thinking acorns should produce oaks overnight.

God *could* produce instant oaks if it were His perfect will for acorns. Some plants He does grow up overnight, and sometimes He *does* produce instant healing for people because that is His perfect answer for them, given their circumstances.

But there are other equally miraculous answers. We just fail to recognize them because they are not spectacular or they don't square with what we expected. Here we must lay down another basic principle. *God doesn't always provide the answer we desire or expect, but He always honors our faith!*

A naive farmer may be perturbed when it snows on his wheat, but soon he will learn that the snow is a blanket protecting the crop from freezing. That is illustrative of the way God deals with His children.

There is no way God's children can have a deep, profound faith in Him until they can believe He honors their faith with many, many different — and often unexpected— answers. Different, yes, but always *better*.

My friend Robert Stamps tells an intriguing story of how

God always answers our faith-prayers, and in unexpected ways. Let's allow him to relate it in his own words.

"I have a friend who was a chaplain in the Philippines during World War II. One day he and his platoon became separated from their company and were trapped behind Japanese lines. A dense fog settled over the entire jungle, and for a week it kept them from going anywhere. At any moment they expected to be discovered by the Japanese, and they were all scared to death.

"Finally, my chaplain friend knelt with his platoon all around and prayed, 'God, lift this hideous fog so that we can get out of the jungle and back to our own lines.'

"Five minutes later, guess what happened? The fog did not lift, but they heard voices . . . Japanese voices. Slowly the platoon maneuvered around the voices from the Japanese lines, and, hidden by the fog, they worked their way back to the American lines.

"The fog did not lift when my friend prayed, but did God hear his prayer? You bet! He heard, 'Father, help us get back to our own lines.' God heard the prayer, offered in humble faith, and answered in a *better* way than the pray-er had asked. If the fog had lifted, they would have been visible to the enemy."[3]

Having made God's prerogatives clear, we may go on to some examples of the different ways in which God honors faith. Let's examine one of God's most spectacular responses: those that occur when He answers instantly.

In the New Testament account, almost every one of the miracles of healing Jesus performed took place instantly. The blind were given sight; the paralytics were made mobile; the lepers were cleansed. The epileptics, the demon-possessed, the physically deformed—all were restored instantly.

The ten lepers (see Luke 17:12–19) were exceptions. They cried out to Jesus, and He told them to show themselves to the priest. The Bible says they were healed "as they went." We don't know if they went a mile or a hundred yards, but the story would seem to indicate that they hadn't gone very far. They were healed almost instantly, we know that for sure.

God still honors faith instantly today. I said in the first chapter that the only people who don't believe in instant healing are the people who haven't experienced it. I was healed instantly at the age of four. I have told the story elsewhere,[4] but it bears repeating here.

I contracted a disease of the kidneys called nephritis, in which there is a complete stoppage of the kidneys. My little body swelled to almost twice its normal size, and my temperature soared to astronomical heights. In those days the doctors had neither antibiotics nor great bypass kidney machines to wash and purify the blood. About the only medicine available was quinine, so I was given huge doses of it day after day. Sometimes I think I can still taste the bitterness in my mouth.

The days passed until finally one night after supper, the doctor came to visit. He examined me in my room, then said to my preacher-father, "Jim, if there's anything you want to say or do for this boy, you'd better be doing it. He won't be here in the morning."

Father said, "Have you done all you know to do? Isn't there something else?"

The kindly old doctor shook his white head sadly and

said, "There's nothing more we can do, Jim. Nothing."

Father looked at the floor for a long moment, with all the anguish in his heart that only a pronouncement like that could bring. Then he looked up and said, "Well, doctor, there's something more *I* can do."

He turned and went down the hall to another bedroom, where he fell to his knees at the side of the bed. (Father *always* prayed on his knees, whether he was in the pulpit, at Rotary Club, or wherever—it didn't matter.) That night he prayed something like this: "O God, I don't have to tell You how dearly I love this boy, for You had a Son once and You know. Dear God, I know You love him more than I. Lord, if You want to take him You can have him, for I know he'll be far better off in heaven than here."

Then he went on, "But Lord, if in Your infinite wisdom and mercy You spare his life, I promise to do everything humanly possible to see that his life is given to You in service. Nevertheless, not my will but Thine be done."

Moments after his prayer was completed, the doctor flung open the door and shouted, "Jim, come quickly!"

Together they rushed into the room where I lay. Liquids were pouring from every pore in my body; the sheets and my pajamas were drenched as my fever broke. In a few moments my temperature was normal once more, and by morning the long road to full strength and health had begun.

Now where was the *faith* in that? Was it in a bargain struck between my father and God? Did my father say "Okay, God, I've done my part, now you do Yours"? Did the faith lie in the act of prayer?

I submit that what faith there was in that prayer, was the

faith born of desperation, when the last human choice (which was to beg and plead) was surrendered (perhaps *relinquished* is a better word) to the wisdom, mercy, and complete knowledge of a loving God. In this case faith lay in the relinquishment, and God honored that faith instantly with a spectacular miracle. The relinquishment probably set Him free from His self-limitation to do what He wanted to do, but of course I am not certain.

However, in no way did my father's faith change God's mind, persuade Him to do something He hadn't thought of, or cause Him to be willing to do something He had heretofore been reluctant to do. Why then did God honor faith by an instant healing? I *believe* it was because that was the best answer under the circumstances. I do not *know*, and neither does anyone else. As the prophet said so profoundly long ago,

> For my thoughts are not your
> thoughts,
> neither are your ways my ways,
> says the LORD (Is. 55:8).

The following, by contrast, is a case where faith was honored by God in a completely unexpected way, and in God's eyes, at least, a way which was far better than the request. Grace was a lovely woman in her early forties. She belonged to our church and was an active participant in its program. She was an eager servant of God in any way she was asked. Serving people seemed to be her joy.

The church was profoundly shocked and deeply grieved when we learned that she had cancer. The doctor had pronounced it terminal. She went physically downhill at a rapid rate and, as I prayed for her, it seemed to me God was saying, *Have a service of prayer in her behalf.*

Those were the days when such a thing was unheard of in my particular denomination. Those were also the days when what people thought mattered a lot more to me than it does now. (Glory! It's great to be free!) The situation was a real problem for me. I argued and rationalized and pleaded with the Lord, but He would not let me out of it.

Finally the Holy Spirit had His way and, once I had made the decision, I felt inwardly relieved and very, very excited. The announcement was duly made that on Friday night a service of prayer for the sick would be held. Everyone knew it was primarily for Grace and, to my astonishment (which reveals how little faith *I* had), the church was almost filled.

The service was beautiful and powerful. The Spirit of God came down and caught us up in wave after wave of love and assurance. When the service ended, I went to the home of Grace and her family. I had told them I was coming and they were expecting me.

Grace was up, though weak and thin, and sitting in a rocking chair. I enthusiastically told them of the love the people had shown her and of the power there had been in the service. "And now, Grace," I said, "I am going to pray for you."

I went around behind her, laid my hands on her head, and prayed from the very depths of my heart that God would heal her. I prayed with all the faith I could muster. That night as I went home, my heart was singing.

In a matter of weeks Grace was healed, but not in the way I had prayed. She was healed in her homecoming in heaven. After the funeral I went out to the house with her husband and teen-aged son. Roger told me what had happened the night of the prayer service.

"We had never been able to talk about Grace's illness," he said. "From the moment of diagnosis until that night, we had all three been playing games with one another, pretending there was nothing wrong. But after you left, all the barriers fell down. The next morning we got out the Bible and began family prayers each day. Our family will never be any more unified and blessed, until we all are in heaven, than it has been these past few weeks."

Whoever would say that was not an answer to a prayer for healing needs to learn a crucial lesson. There are healings other than those of the flesh. Grace's story is a classic example of having faith for one petition but receiving from God a different and better blessing, including the healing of a family relationship.

We are dealing mostly with physical healing in this chapter for two reasons: first, because of the intense interest in Christian circles just now and, second, because physical healing is *visible* and therefore undeniable. But there is another kind of healing that takes place as a result of faith prayers, and that happens when the Spirit of God performs a *remedial* (i.e., using medicines) miracle.

When our son was a tiny baby, he contracted a bad cold. The sickness progressed until one night the coughing, wheezing, and high temperature drove us to call the doctor. He said, "It sounds like pneumonia to me. You had better bring him in."

We drove the three miles to the village that night with our only child bundled warmly and apprehension gripping our hearts. We prayed that God would lay His healing hand upon the child; never did two people pray more earnestly.

When we arrived at the doctor's office he examined the child and confirmed his over-the-phone diagnosis. "I'm going to try a new drug that is sweeping the medical community in this country," he said. "They're having outstanding success with it. It comes from England."

That night there was a drastic change. You could almost watch the fever diminish and the flush leave our son's cheeks. By morning the fever was gone. We exuberantly called the doctor to report as he had requested. We didn't forget to thank God, either. "By the way," I asked, "what was the name of that new drug?"

"Penicillin," he replied. God enacted a miracle using a doctor and medicine.

Sometimes taking an aspirin tablet can be the most spiritual act a human being can perform. Look, God's remedies are *all* miracles. Every well-balanced Bible teacher recognizes that God is the author of all healing.

If medicine is the vehicle God uses, the cure is still God's miracle. That is why Oral Roberts, for instance, has built his hospital, the City of Faith—not so God can heal people with medicine in the event prayer fails, but so that prayer and medicine might work together as one. God will use both as He sees fit.

Whoever tries to separate the sacred from the secular needs to see that *all* creation is of God. The "secular" is not some kind of a category which God separated from the creation after He brought it into being. "The earth is the LORD's and the fulness thereof . . . " (Ps. 24:1).

Let me depart from the subject of healing for a moment to address another kind of faith request. I want to lend a word of encouragement to those who have children of marriageable age and who are deeply troubled about their choice of a companion. To say this is a matter of grave concern to Christian parents of teen-agers today is putting it mildly. Seeing children through this decision is a real burden.

I believe with all my heart that God participates in this choice and that He honors the faith of those who cling to Him. How can a person find the one who is "right"? Do we meet our mates by "chance"? Is God in the "who-to-marry" business?

It stands to reason, if God is the founder of the institution of marriage He is concerned about preserving it. He will do everything necessary to provide the suitable mate if we will exercise free choice and allow Him. But it takes faith, and faith is what He honors. Here is a story of the healing of longing.

Our daughter became a Christian at the age of ten, but she became a Spirit-filled, excited Christian when she was a sophomore in college. One of the first vows she made at that point was that she would not marry a man unless he was a Christian.

As the years passed she upgraded her requirement a bit. "He must be a 'turned-on' Christian. Otherwise he won't understand when I want to go to Bible-study groups and have friends in to share Christ," she said.

The years went by, and she dated many young men. None seemed to meet the standard she had set. She prayed earnestly and, of course, we joined her in our own daily prayers. Our prayer was "Lord, lead her to the right one."

Judy reached the age of twenty-six, the age when most women begin to entertain fleeting thoughts of "What if I don't meet him?" and feel flashes of panic. But she prayed on, firm and unshakeable in her faith that God would lead her to the right person.

One day in the June of her twenty-sixth year she called and was a bit "down." She said plaintively, "I'm lonely and tired of living by myself. I wish God would hurry a bit." Then with resolute certainty she said, "I know God has him out there somewhere, and he's been made just for me."

A month passed. One Sunday night a young man walked into the church services Judy attended. He was a stranger—tall, handsome, clean-cut, and smiling. Judy's heart leaped.

The pastor called for prayertime at the altar and, as she knelt, she prayed, "Lord, I'm not going to be pushy. If he's the one, you're going to have to arrange the meeting."

As she prayed, she felt a tap on her shoulder. An elderly lady stood there smiling. "Judy," she said, "this is Ed. I wanted you two to meet."

That was it. Ed turned out to be the "right one." How he does love God. After several years they are still radiantly happy, with lovely children.

Later Ed told us that he had determined to marry only an excited Christian, and he too was praying that God would lead him to the "right one." In June that year he said the Holy Spirit let him know that the time was drawing near. He began to build a new house for the Christian bride he knew by faith he would soon meet.

In November they spent their wedding night in the house God had told him to build! God is a miracle-working God, and He honors the faith of His children. When His will turns out to be the same as theirs, He gives them exactly what they desire and true happiness results.

At times, however, the greatest answer God can give is

no. That answer honors faith by calling for more faith. I can think of no better example than Moses. Remember the story?

The Israelites ran out of water, and they began to complain and browbeat Moses for having led them from Egypt into such a mess. Moses went off with Aaron to pray about it, and God told Moses to speak to a giant rock and water would come forth.

But instead of speaking to the rock, Moses struck it with his staff. The water rushed forth, but God told Moses that, as a result of his disobedience, he could not enter the Promised Land (see Num. 20:12).

At this point Moses could have said, "That does it, I've had it with religion! Look at what I have done for Him. I left the great palace in Egypt with all its comforts. I risked my neck by confronting Pharaoh several times. I led them from bondage to freedom and now, because of one little slip, God has denied me the greatest desire of my life. Serving God doesn't pay, so forget it!"

Many people retreat into bitterness and cynicism when their heart's desires are frustrated; Moses could have done the same. Yet there is no record that Moses complained or uttered one negative word. Instead, he went about the business God had called him to do and, for the next forty years, led the Israelites through the most trying years of their history as they wandered in the wilderness. It took a great faith to respond like that!

God can honor faith by saying no and that almost always calls for a still greater faith in Him. The other choice, of course, is that we harden our hearts and rebel.

Other times He honors faith by simply saying, "I'll make you adequate." That is what He said to Paul. Paul had a problem. We don't know exactly what it was, but the biblical evidence indicates it was probably some physical ailment that pained him constantly.

Paul was a man of faith if ever there was one. Yet when he asked God to deliver him from this problem, (not once, but three times!) God said, ". . .'My grace is sufficient for you . . .' " (2 Cor. 12:9).

Why didn't God give Paul his heart's desire? All things being equal, couldn't God better use a strong, healthy Paul than one beset with a plaguing illness? Paul could have rebelled, gotten angry, even abandoned his faith. Pain has made other people do so.

I don't know why God didn't heal Paul. I do know that His answer called forth from the apostle greater faith than ever—faith in a God who would make him able and adequate and give him a life of great victory. This is the same kind of faith out of which Job cried, "Though he slay me, yet will I trust in him . . . " (Job 13:15 KJV).

It takes a special faith, when the bottom falls out of life and all our dreams lie in shattered bits about us, to believe that God has a better answer for us than the one we had in mind. When God's children respond to Him with that kind of faith, He *always* honors it in a way that is ultimately greater than the disappointment and pain out of which their faith had sprung. From beginning to end, the Bible teaches us how enormously important it is to learn to trust God. He is the Alpha and the Omega of every circumstance.

A long time ago I read the best definition of faith I have ever seen. An evangelist was relating an experience where he went into the ghettos of Chicago, to visit a little church which a great compassionate man had founded. He was asked to teach a Sunday school class comprised of a few small boys who had been born in the slums and had grown up in that sordid area.

The evangelist was trying to teach the boys the meaning of faith. He held up a silver dollar and announced, "I am going to give this dollar to one of you boys." Their eyes widened with disbelief. Most of them had never seen a silver dollar before.

He started around the circle and held out the dollar to the first little boy. "Here, take it," he said. All his life the boy had known nothing but angry bullying, beatings, disappointments, and hurt from grown-ups. It was beyond the capacity of his little mind to believe that someone would offer a gift so precious with no strings attached. Surely there must be a catch somewhere—he would have to suffer as always if he took it. He drew back and shook his head negatively.

Around the circle the evangelist went. One after another the boys refused until, finally, one little boy found the courage to lift his grimy hand timidly and take the dollar. Then he quickly looked up, as if expecting a blow or a reprimand. The evangelist only smiled and said, "You may keep it, son. It's yours—a gift from me."

He turned to the class and said, "Faith is just taking what God is offering you . . . no questions asked."

And so it is. Your heavenly Father knows your needs, and He has promised to meet them. More than that, in every circumstance of your life He offers you answers that will astound you. His mercy, gifts, and love will thrill you through and through. He is a great, generous, powerful God.

But He can never give you what you refuse to receive.

35

III

The Faith Promises
in the Bible—
Can We Count on Them?

Faith is not looking out into the darkness and saying, "It is light outside." Faith is looking out into the darkness and saying, "It will be light soon." Faith is not the contradiction of reality; it is a simple trust in the Lord of reality.

When I was a small boy, I remember lying in bed one dark summer night and listening to the sounds of singing, crying, and agonizing prayers. Those sounds came from a house across the way in which a little boy lay near death. Playing in the garage earlier in the day, he had discovered a pop bottle and had drunk a large amount of the contents. Tragically, it had been filled with coal oil.

The parents of the child did not seek medical attention, but at once called members of their church. The elders and their families gathered and began a prayer vigil by the bedside of the stricken child.

Throughout the night their hymns and prayers rent the air. They shouted the great promises recorded in the Bible. They reminded God of what His Word said and, in the name of Jesus, they claimed healing for the child. But to no avail. Toward daylight the soul of the child slipped out of his body and winged his way to be with God forever.

A wave of anger swept through the community. Indignant mainline church members talked of warrants and arrests for a few days, but then life went on and the incident was forgotten.

I wonder if the parents forgot. Their faith was very deep and very simple. The Bible specifically promised that, if one asked God for anything and believed, one would receive. They did not wish to deny the Bible. They could only blame themselves for lacking sufficient faith, and the result must have been agonizing guilt and self-condemnation.

That was years ago. Today similar teaching is growing into a huge movement. "Faith teachers" are numerous in almost every community throughout the land. A common term associated with this group is the "full-faith movement." Their belief is that, because the Bible seems to promise it, a person may obtain any answer from God he desires—provided he has enough faith. "Enough" faith is presumed to be the amount you possessed if you obtained your expected answer.

I have said before that what a person believes about faith tells me the kind of God in whom he believes. The God of these dear people is virtually predictable. He works by automation and by rote. One's faith sets the "Master mechanism" in action. Their God honors prayer *always* and *only* according to the amount of faith He finds.

The extremists in this movement will tell you that, if you go to a doctor, take medicine, own insurance policies, seek any form of security in the world, or make any provision for future calamity, you are guilty of doubting the power of God.

Of course, there are moderates and conservatives within this movement, too, and fortunately they far outnumber the extremists. But even among the moderates, guilt and self-condemnation run rampant when prayer "fails" in some great crisis situation. Since they cannot blame the Bible, they must always blame themselves.

Let me repeat again, I am not putting down these teachers. I am not looking down my nose at them. As Christians we are on the same team, and our mutual desire is to exalt Jesus Christ. Many wonderful miracles have resulted from this movement. That is because God has always had to use imperfect shepherds with his sheep. Who is the perfect teacher among us?

Much of the other teaching of the movement is (in my opinion) basically sound. My objection is to the distorted view of God that claims He answers prayer *only* on the basis of faith. This view brings great pain and does great damage to the people of the Lord. A god who is limited to answering prayers only according to faith is less than the God revealed by Jesus Christ.

Recently a dear friend of mine became a cancer victim. He came to me in deep distress. His physician had advised him to go to a certain medical center for chemotherapy treatment. As he was preparing to go, a few of his relatives who were members of the full-faith movement came to see him. They told him he did not need to seek medical assistance; if he did, it would be an insult to God. Complete faith, they said, would bring about a complete healing because the Word of God promised it.

When he came to see me, he was in inner torment. He loved God devoutly. Yet he loved his relatives, too, and had great faith in their commitment. After a long talk and considerable prayer together, he decided to go ahead with the treatment. That has been many, many months ago, and today he is operating efficiently again, physically strong and happy.

Scotti is a devout Christian friend who underwent a very traumatic experience some time ago. Her father was stricken with a rare blood disease at age forty-nine. Another of his daughters was not a Christian, and he was deeply concerned. One day he made the statement that it might take his death to bring her to see her need.

His wife asked, "Would you be willing to die for that?"

"I believe that I would," he replied.

He was in the hospital only three weeks before his death. Later, Scotti was approached by one of her acquaintances who was a follower of a well-known faith teacher. After she had heard the details she told Scotti, "Your father was killed by Satan. There must have been sin in his life, so when he confessed he was willing to die for his daughter, it freed Satan to take his life. You and your mother could have saved his life if you had claimed a promise and stood on it."

Would my friend have been instantly healed without chemotherapy if he had had "more faith"? Would Scotti's father have been healed if she and her mother had had "more faith"? Did both my friend and Scotti doubt the validity of the Scriptures? I don't think so.

This brings us to look at a few of the great faith promises in the Bible, to examine them in depth, and to suggest alternate ways of viewing them. First, I need to make one thing clear: My entire life is based on my experience with God and His Word. I am neither a Bible skeptic *nor* a scholarly critic of the Scriptures. I believe that the Holy Bible is the inspired record of the revelation of God through Jesus Christ—and I trust that that statement will help the reader to know exactly where "I am coming from" (bad English—good communication).

You are going to have to get your Bible so we can study along together. So I'll wait a moment.

Okay, let's begin. Here is the first promise we shall tackle.

1. . . . with his stripes we are healed (Is. 53:5 KJV).

The magnificent fifty-third chapter of Isaiah describes the atonement of Jesus Christ seven hundred and fifty years before it happened. By the Atonement, I mean at Calvary Jesus Christ bridged the gulf between our sinfulness and God's holiness, so that whoever receives Jesus Christ as Lord and Savior is no longer separated from God but *at one* with Him now and forevermore.

This passage makes it clear that Jesus died for our sins and our sicknesses. There is no way one can separate sin from physical disease in the Atonement. The Hebrew word for "healed" is *rapha* and has only one meaning: physical healing. Jesus did indeed die for our sins and our sicknesses.

The full-faith school of thought teaches that, when we call upon God for salvation, we are saved instantly. They also teach that, when a physical malady comes upon us and we call upon God for healing, we are healed instantly, for Jesus bore all our sins and all our sicknesses on the cross. Our part of the transaction is to receive healing by faith.

If we waver, it is a sign of a lack of faith in the atoning death of Jesus Christ Himself. Therefore, we are blocking God. If symptoms of sickness persist, we are to ignore them.

Now let me present another point of view. Notice I did not say "the right answer." I am not a spiritual data bank with the definitive, final answer to everything. The Holy Spirit is my teacher, and He isn't finished with me yet. What I am offering is an alternate point of view which I believe does not limit or block God. It does not pooh-pooh the holy Word of God either.

I believe it is true that God grants salvation when He is asked and that our status in His eyes changes instantly. In that moment it has been decided that sin and death shall have no ultimate claim on us; through Jesus Christ they have been defeated. We are to march on with God with the understanding that the ultimate outcome has been decided.

But this does not mean that we cannot commit sin again. In fact the Scripture assumes that we will when it says, ". . . if ["when" is implied] any man sin, we have an advocate with the Father . . ." (1 John 2:1 KJV).

Likewise, it is literally true that "with his stripes we are healed," for on Calvary's cross it was decided once and for all that sickness shall not have the ultimate claim upon us or finally overcome us. Jesus regarded sickness and evil as a part of the kingdom of darkness. The Scripture makes that crystal clear:

> "And ought not this woman, a daughter of Abraham
> whom Satan bound for eighteen years, be loosed from
> this bond on the sabbath day?" (Luke 13:16).

Thus sin and sickness are of Satan. Although Jesus dealt with them on Calvary, this *does not mean* that, after we receive Jesus Christ, we shall never be sick again.

To me it means that the ultimate outcome has been decided and that just as God forgives each sin as we commit them on an individual basis, so he deals with each "sick spell" that we might have on an individual basis. He *always* forgives sin personally because that is always the best possible answer, and He has chosen to deal with sickness on a case-by-case basis. One day both will be eradicated. He did not heal Paul instantly when Paul asked. In his case, that did not seem to God to be the best possible answer. He allowed the "thorn," but He provided enough grace to assure victory.

Yes, "with his stripes we are healed." Let us rejoice in that healing, praise God for it, and ask for the specific application of it to ourselves and to others as each case comes along. The enemy has been overcome. In our specific case the sickness will be healed physically if, out of the love and wisdom of God Almighty, healing is the best possible answer for us.

2. Ask, and it will be given you. . . . (Matt. 7:7).

At the age of eight I learned Matthew 7:7 in Sunday school. I had been taught that the Bible was true.

The one thing I wanted more than anything else in the world was a shotgun. I longed for a shotgun. I thought heaven would come down if only I could rest my cheek on the cool wood of its stock and curl my little eight-year-old fingers around the cold steel of its barrel. With all the childlike faith an eight-year-old can have, I asked God for a shotgun.

I didn't receive it. I was baffled and, in fact, I thought it was a bit tacky for God to treat me this way. But I know something now I didn't know then. Both God and my father loved me too much to grant my request. They knew that I wasn't old enough or wise enough to handle it and that I might do great harm to myself or others. And, may I add, when I reached the proper age my father gave me a shotgun of my very own.

God is not a God who furnishes us with an endless supply of blank checks. We are not assured that He will sign them and give us everything on demand. No, instead we must submit to His will.

My dear full-faith friends are inclined to see all the faith promises as blank checks that *we* fill out and sign. They become the means by which, if we have enough faith in the bank, we can always procure exactly what we want.

How then do we view the precious promise that states if we ask we shall receive? A look at biblical chain references will lead us to James, where this "ask" promise is expanded.

Remember the disciple James is writing (under inspiration) after he has had the plan of salvation explained to him by Jesus Himself, after he and the other disciples had been gloriously filled with the Holy Spirit. The Holy Spirit had brought the teachings of Jesus to his "remembrance" (John 14:26), and we find James expounding on this promise concerning asking and receiving.

> . . . You do not have, because you do not ask. You ask and do not receive, because you ask wrongly, to spend it on your passions (James 4:2,3).

Now let me ask a serious question. Is it fair to quote the second verse without the third? To do so, in my opinion, is to take the promise out of context and mislead the asker. Many of the miracle-on-demand people quote verse two without quoting verse three, thus furthering the idea of a blank-check God.

James seems to be stating that God sometimes says, "I must refuse your request because your motives are wrong. You want it for reasons that are less than my desire for you, so I will withhold the answer you want. I love you too much to let you settle for less than the best."

We can only conclude that it is possible for us to block God by wrong motives when we ask and that, even if our motives are pure, he always reserves the right to exercise His best choice in the matter. That is the way any mighty king and loving father operates. And our God does so too—perfectly.

We are to pray and trust God. We are to claim God's promises and agree with them. We are to believe God will do what He says He will do. Great faith always believes that God will act from His vantage point of knowing all things. The only limitation that can ever be placed on any promise of the Father is that God is too good to grant us everything we ask Him in every situation. That is the kind of limitation I can live with *forever*!

3. . . . *Have faith in God. Truly, I say to you, whoever says to this mountain, 'Be taken up and cast into the sea,' and does not doubt in his heart, but believes that what he says will come to pass, it will be done for him. Therefore I tell you, whatever you ask in prayer, believe that you have received it, and it will be yours (Mark 11:22–24).*

The promise of Mark 11 occurs right after the incident of the withered fig tree. The disciples were awestricken when Jesus uttered this promise.

Jesus delighted in speaking in hyperbole, dramatizing and exaggerating a figure of speech to make His point. The

45

most famous example of that is when He admonished us to amputate our hand or pluck out our eye if it causes us to sin (see Matt. 5:30).

Obviously He was using hyperbole here. This promise is definitely not a blank check, nor is it unconditional. He had to be speaking figuratively to make a point; otherwise, with as many Christians as there are who believe God's promises, the Rocky Mountains would be moved by faith and scattered all over the earth. Can't you see it? Pike's Peak in Arkansas, Mt. Rainier in North Dakota!

Not only that, if this promise were literally true, surely some great spiritual giant would have moved Mount St. Helens to the middle of the Pacific Ocean when it erupted. After all, it tragically brought death and destruction to many in a wide area.

Here some people will protest, "You do not believe the Bible. Jesus said we are to have faith. God's promises are unconditional."

Well, as a matter of fact, this particular promise is *very* conditional. We hear very little about it from the full-faith folks when they begin claiming this promise to obtain from God what they want. The condition lies in the very next verse. Remember, Christ is explaining how He was able to cause the fig tree to wither. He is instructing them in praying for miracles, and He says:

> And whenever you stand praying, forgive, if you have anything against any one; so that your Father also who is in heaven may forgive you your trespasses (Mark 11:25).

He is saying plainly that there are conditions or impediments in our lives that can block God. He names one, which implies there may be others. When you add this to the facts that God is a good God, He says no when He wants to give us something better, and He denies our petitions for our greater good, what you have left is not a blank-check God but a mighty, loving, heavenly Father.

Again the cry arises, "You are downgrading the Bible." No, I am upgrading our understanding of God.

It is not a cop-out or self-righteousness to say that the Bible *seems* to say a certain thing to us, but as we grow and mature in our understanding we see newer and deeper things. We can say, "Now, why didn't I see that? I have read that passage a thousand times and have never seen that before." It was probably because you finally grew to the point the Holy Spirit could reveal it to you. Haven't you had that happen? Whoever buries himself in the Word of God finds the process happening over and over again. Jesus Himself said to His disciples: " 'I have yet many things to say to you, but you cannot bear them now. When the Spirit of truth comes, he will guide you into all the truth . . .' " (John 16:12,13).

4. *Whatever you ask in my name, I will do it, that the Father may be glorified in the Son; if you ask anything in my name, I will do it (John 14:13,14).*

John 14:13 is another "ask" promise, and it is also one of the "name-it-and-claim-it" promises. Although we are not told, I am very sure that it was burning in the mind of Peter as he and John were going to the temple to pray soon after Pentecost.

They came to a lame man at the gate of the temple, and

he asked them for alms. Peter was moved with compassion and said, ". . .'I have no silver and gold, but I give you what I have; in the name of Jesus of Nazareth, walk' " (Acts 3:6). The lame man was healed; he arose and began to dance for joy.

There are several other promises in which we are invited to ask in the name of Jesus. But all of them are conditional in that we are instructed to ask in the name of Jesus.

One prominent faith teacher was speaking on the authority of believers. He said that we do not realize the power of "the Name," and he quoted this verse:

> Therefore God has highly exalted him and bestowed
> on him the name which is above every name (Phil.
> 2:9).

Then he said, "The name of Jesus is above every name. Cancer is a name, heart disease is a name, every disease has a name. Jesus' name is above them all. Believers should use that name with authority, for it is theirs to use."

People left the meeting understanding that the believer could take the name of Jesus and use it like a divine laser beam. Fire it into any disease, and the affliction would sizzle and disappear.

There certainly is power in the name of Jesus Christ, and believers are commanded to call upon the name of the Lord. But the name of Jesus Christ is not black magic whereby we decide we can deal with any and all situations in the complete assurance that we are doing the perfect will of God.

To ask in the name of Jesus Christ means to *ask*—according to who Jesus Christ is and according to God's will. If I "ask wrongly, to spend it on [my] passions [cove-tous desires]" as James observed (4:3), am I using the precious name of Christ? If I am using that name to ask for something that ultimately is not in the best interest of the kingdom of God, is God going to wilt in His purpose just because I phonetically uttered the Name?

We need to use the name of Jesus when we pray; we can only approach the Father "through Jesus Christ our Lord." There *is* power when we pray in that name, but not to rule as little gods over every situation that arises. To believe that is to worship the Name itself. The power and the decision as to its use lie in the One who bears that name.

5. *Again I say to you, if two of you agree on earth about anything they ask, it will be done for them by my Father in heaven (Matt. 18:19).*

In Matthew 18:19 there is a promise which appears to be almost unconditional—no reservations, no hidden meanings, just plain simple everyday language that tells us we can have anything we want. The only condition attached is that two of us should be in agreement.

Yet we know that in our practical application of this promise, even though we fulfill the single condition and agree, things don't always turn out the way we have asked.

Let me use the example (a true case) of a man who broke his false teeth. He read that nothing was impossible with God, so he and his wife decided they would not go to the expense of a new set of teeth. They claimed Matthew 18:19 and waited. Nothing happened.

I do not intend to poke fun at these dear earnest people, but I use this rather ludicrous example to dramatize that

God is God and we are human. We are never going to have faith enough to get Him to deny His nature, surrender all His options, or pray Him into giving us less than the best for us. Most important, He is not going to climb down from His throne and let us sit in His seat. He let us have our own way once, and we crucified Him!

I am not downgrading God's Word or faith promises. Here is another example from the present moment. Less than a week ago this very promise of Matthew 18:19 became flesh in our household.

My wife Martha has a touch of arthritis in her spine, a condition which has shortened some of her back muscles. Consequently, when she "overdoes it," works in an unnatural position, or becomes overly tired, those muscles begin a series of spasms that throw her into excruciating agony. Only those who have experienced that particular pain can know how it feels. A doctor told me it produces a pain level as high as any known to the medical profession.

At 3 A.M. a few days ago Martha awakened in agony. The spasms had begun. No more sleep that night—nothing but pain, pain, pain. Talking was such an effort I could barely hear her voice. I sat on the edge of the bed, laid my hands on her, and prayed with all the faith and earnestness at my command for God to heal her.

We had planned to call our son Ken, who lives in Florida, that morning. I asked if she still wanted to call. She said yes, so I brought an extension phone for her and went downstairs to make the call.

After a brief visit, I explained to Ken that his mother was in such terrific pain she was scarcely able to move. I told him I had already prayed for her healing and asked if he would do the same.

Over the telephone Ken prayed the prayer of faith, claimed the promise, and entrusted his mother into God's hands in as simple and sincere a way as possible.

In a moment or two Martha came from the bedroom and said with joy, "Oh, I'm much better. I believe God has healed me!"

He had! No doubt about it. That morning she dusted the entire house and scrubbed the bathtub. That was Saturday. Sunday was Father's Day and we had a wonderful day together. This morning (Monday) she walked the usual four miles with me, praising God and rejoicing in His goodness.

What happened? Such an event is easy to rationalize. Perhaps it was the psychology of her only son in prayer for her that relaxed Martha's muscles and set her free—that is what some would say. Why do we feel that, if we can explain a miracle, God didn't have anything to do with it?

I do not believe that explanation for a moment, but even if it is true, the miracle is not diminished. *All* healing is from God. To believe otherwise is to separate the sacred from the secular and that, in reality, is impossible.

The best explanation, in my opinion, is that we applied the prayer and the promise. "Two of us" —my son and I— agreed, and our Father "who is in heaven" healed Martha because in this situation, according to His divine knowledge, it was the best possible answer. At other times, we had prayed the same prayer, and Martha had had to "wear out" the pain—usually for a week to ten days.

Well, then, does God play favorites? Does He keep a "most popular" list? Has this discussion been a cop-out? Does Martha's healing mean that we cannot select one of the promises of God and apply it to our situation? Does it mean Jesus didn't really mean it when He said we could ask anything from the Father and we would receive it? Does it mean that all the faith promises are just symbolic, and we should not take them seriously?

No, No, NO!

We must have such an understanding of the promises of God that we won't make the mistake of trying to make magic formulas out of them. They are not gimmicks whereby we hem God in, so that He has no way out but our way.

The promises of God are not dead, cold formulas; they are living possibilities! The Bible is the *living Word*. It has been decided that sin and sickness would not ultimately destroy us, but that the Holy Spirit would work His truth personally in us and with us and for us because of Calvary. We may lay hold of these promises and base our petitions on them. God will always answer. There are times, and situations, when God's answer is, indeed, what our hearts desire. The Holy Spirit acts as we expected, and the answer happens!

Let me sum up what I have been trying to say by this illustration. Let us compare the Bible to a pocket calculator, programmed by the manufacturer, who is, of course, God the Father. Suppose that I am a person with a very limited education. And suppose I am a slow learner; some lessons I must learn over and over again. I especially have problems with math. But someone has given me a calculator which they said would answer all my questions about math.

One day I want to know the sum of 3 plus 3. I press the buttons, but because of my limited knowledge about the calculator and about numbers, I press 3 plus 2 instead of 3 plus 3. The calculator comes up with the answer 5. The calculator is not mistaken. I am mistaken, for I am presuming that I know how to operate my calculator. I presume that both the calculator and I are correct, so I trust that the answer is 5.

Obviously from then on, unless I learn more about numbers and calculators I am going to operate my life under the conviction that 3 plus 3 is 5. That means the rest of my life I am going to have a messed-up checkbook, receive nasty letters from the IRS and the charge card people, and have all sorts of problems. I will spend my life defending my faith in my calculator because I believe it has told me that the sum of 3 plus 3 is 5.

(We cannot push this illustration any further. If we did, we would have to assume that by our learning to press the correct faith buttons God must give us the answer we want. This twists truth, and we end up with a big chunk of the forbidden fruit in our mouths. We think we know "good and evil," God is completely predictable, and we are in firm control. God is reduced to a panel light which blinks dutifully at our faith command.)

We can push the illustration as far as we like *if we make God the operator*. He programmed the calculator; He has perfect knowledge of how to operate it. We can trust Him to give us not only the best possible answer but the *right* one.

Because he knows instantly the complete programming of the instrument and the full consequences of his answer, if we ask, "Lord, what is 3 plus 3?" He will never say, "The correct answer is 5.999999." That would be close to the truth, but not true. God's answer will always be "6," for out of all the possible answers programmed into the calculator, that is the only one that is highest and true, and so, best for us.

It is true that we cannot force God to do our will by calling up so much faith He cannot resist. But He will act at times as a result of our faith, and we may be certain about that. Furthermore, we can know for sure when He is saying yes. Now you are asking, "But how? How can I be certain?"

That is precisely what we are going to examine next.

IV

How Can I Know
When God is Saying Yes?

It happened every year. I would tell the children in the church membership classes that God loved them and that they could know this for sure. Inevitably one of them would ask, "But how can we know God loves us?"

Then I would ask, "How do you know your mother loves you?"

The little hands would go up instantly. "Because she cooks for me, she washes my clothes, reads stories to me, hugs me when I'm hurt, and curls my hair when I'm going to a party!"

Then I would say, "Those are all nice things. But they are things anybody could do for you whether they loved you or not. Right? So then, how do you know for sure your mother loves you?"

Little puzzled looks, puckered brows, bewilderment, deep thinking. Then a small hand would go up, "Well—well, I just know it, that's all!"

And I would say, "That's the right answer!" You just know. Beyond that, there are no words.

There are no words beyond that because that is the only way anyone ever knows he or she is loved. This is true because there are no words that ultimately describe love. Love is something you know by *experiencing* it.

That is also the only way you can know God is speaking to you. There are two primary ways in which God speaks to us. The first is through His eternal, inspired Word. The Bible is like a beautiful melody with an obligato. An obligato, of course, is an accompaniment superimposed upon the melody. Played or sung together they make fantastic music. In our analogy the melody is the Bible, the written Word. The obligato is the word quickened to you. In a particular situation the written Word can be set afire, as it were, by the Holy Spirit to become God's personal, directive word for you right where you are. This is the second way in which God speaks. Let me illustrate.

I was converted at the age of ten. Because my father was an evangelical minister, I had heard God's eternal Word many, many times in my young life. But one precious day in a revival meeting the melody of the Word took on an obligato and spoke to me in a life-changing way. I knew that it was for me at that particular time. I was born anew. Can you not relate a similar experience? When you came to Christ, God's eternal Word became His personal word for you. As a Christian, He continues to incorporate truth in your life in this way.

When we feel deeply that God has spoken to us personally, there is one unfailing test we can apply if we want to make certain. *If that personal word does not conform to God's written Word, forget it.* He will never speak a personal word in contradiction to the Holy Scriptures. That would not produce music; an off-key obligato never does. No disciple of Jesus Christ, for example, would ever ask himself,

"Should I commit adultery?" God's Word spells that matter out clearly.

What about this situation? Here is a person living in St. Louis, and he gets a job offer in Detroit. This man and his wife have their circle of friends, their children are happy in school, the work is pleasant in St. Louis, and life is good. Now, along comes this opportunity in Detroit that offers great financial advantage and a chance to upgrade their life-style. What should he do? Go on in the pleasant life that they have, or launch out into that which is unknown but which holds distinct financial promise?

The Bible does not give a clear word about whether people should move from St. Louis to Detroit. The family ponders, prays, computes the scriptural knowledge they have up against the circumstances—and they wait on the guidance of God.

Then one day a conviction stirs up within the man as an artesian well spouts skyward when the driller breaks through limestone. And he *knows*. Perhaps it has come through reading the Psalms or hearing a directive word from his pastor. Maybe he has received a word of wisdom from a close Christian friend. Whatever the case, the Holy Spirit has become the herald of God's will for him. He is to move to Detroit.

Yes, I know that sometimes we agonize in the midnight and *no* answer comes. But remember, in this chapter we are discussing the question, "How can we know when God is saying yes?" We are proceeding on the assumption that we are hearing something.

Let's illustrate this further. Imagine a pipe running over-head, carrying cool water. Cool droplets condense on its

57

outer side, and a drop falls on me. Already I know several things about what has happened. I know the drop is water, for I taste it by touching it to my finger, then to my mouth; I know it is wet and I know that it fell upon me where I was standing.

God's eternal Word flows onward through the pipe of time, but occasionally a special drop of water from it falls upon me. It is water that has condensed in the present environment. It is not actually the water from the inside of the pipe, but it is ultimately from the same source as that in the pipe. And I *know* it is real water. The same Holy Spirit who inspired the Scriptures indwells God's people today.

The possibility for tragedy, disappointment, and despair arises when we take a passage from God's eternal word and try to make of it a personal word to us when, in reality, God has not spoken to us personally. When we hear, and we know, and we obey, great things happen.

A dear Christian friend in Memphis told how she was seated in a restaurant looking out the window when she saw a young man using a pay phone. As he hung up the receiver and turned away she caught a glimpse of stark, stunned despair on his face, and the Holy Spirit said, "Go to him."

She went to him and found that he was a truck driver from Wichita Falls, Texas. There had been a terrible tornado there killing many. His wife and baby were living in a trailer court. He had called the Red Cross about them and had learned the trailer was demolished and his wife and baby were dead.

My friend was able to comfort and minister and help in many, many spiritual and practical ways—as well as to make a great witness to him for the Lord Jesus Christ. She *knew* God had spoken to her, and she obeyed at once.

God has a word for us many, many times out of His loving heart, words that are absolutely consistent with Scripture but cannot be found in His eternal Word, the Bible. When the melody and the obligato are played in harmony, that is when we know we know.

My father tells of his younger sister when their family was still back on the farm. She was stricken with a disease and grew weaker and weaker until they despaired for her life. She could not eat and could scarcely speak because of the terrible weakness in her body.

One day, as the family was about the table at lunch, she called out from an adjoining bedroom, "Mother, didn't Jesus say to a man once, 'Take up thy bed, and walk'?"*

Her mother answered, "Yes, He did."

"Well, He just said that to me!" she replied. She sat up in bed, swung her feet down to the floor, and walked to the table where she ate the first food she had had in days. She never went back to bed because of that illness. It was a clear case of God speaking His eternal Word to her personally at the precise point of her need.

Let me again repeat the caution. The personal word, conveyed by the Holy Spirit, is not something you can conjure up. God speaks to us personally when He desires. My experience has been that it nearly always happens when we least expect it. That is like the Holy Spirit, isn't it? If He is like the wind, who can predict Him? Who knows where the wind will blow or when (see John 3:8)?

Beware. Satan can sometimes convince us God is speaking, especially if we desire something intensely, or if we have made up our minds before we begin to pray. There can

---

*(Mark 2:9 KJV).

be times we want something so badly that we try to trans-
form God's eternal Word into a personal word and claim it.
Inevitably we reap deception and disappointment. It just
doesn't work, even if we find a Bible verse or two to back us
up. We simply must make peace with the fact that God is
going to keep right on being God. We are not going to take
over, force Him, maneuver Him, or intimidate Him with
Scripture, or trap Him into a human formula so that all of
His options are gone and He must give in to us!

When He speaks to us personally, it is always on His
timetable and His terms. This could be very discouraging, if
it were not for the fact that He is a good God, worthy of our
faith and trust in every situation. As I said before, my life is
based on the truth that:

> My thoughts are not your thoughts,
> neither are your ways my ways, says the
> LORD.
> For as the heavens are higher than the
> earth,
> so are my ways higher than your ways,
> and my thoughts than your thoughts
> (Is. 55:8,9).

I intimated a moment ago that a good rule of thumb is, if
the Holy Spirit speaks to us personally at a totally unexpected moment, it can be a hint that it is from the Lord.
Some time ago, four of us were seated in a car outside a
restaurant in a large city in Tennessee. We were preparing
to go into the restaurant for supper prior to worship services. I said to my host, "We will be rushed after supper, so
let's stay here for a moment and have prayer for the services
right now."

At that moment a couple, who we knew were planning to attend the services that night, walked up to the car. I rolled down the window and said, "Get in and have prayer with us for the services tonight."

They got in the car, and I offered prayer. When I finished, the man and his wife burst into tears. Through their sobs he said, "I hope you'll forgive us. But a week ago the doctor found a huge mass in my wife's abdomen, and we are going in the morning to have a further examination and possible surgery. I want you to pray for us."

We all joined hands together. As I began to pray and pour out the desire of our hearts, the obligato to the melody began, the drop of water from the pipe fell upon me, and there arose within me a great inner cell of certainty and absolute assurance of her healing. I began to praise God and thank Him for the miracle He was performing. I claimed one of the great faith promises and closed the prayer with much joy.

The assurance that had come to me was given to them as well and I said without the slightest hesitation, "The doctor won't find that mass there tomorrow. Since this is the last night of the services, I won't see you again. But you needn't write me the results, for I already know them!" They responded with joy and thanksgiving.

Two weeks after I returned home I received a letter from this dear lady. She said, "I know you said I needn't write, but I couldn't keep from it. You were right. Praise God, the next morning when we went for the examination the mass in my abdomen was gone!"

Now, lest you get the idea that that sort of thing happens to me all the time, let me set the record straight. I am not a "faith healer," and I had not really been interested in that aspect of the gospel until the past few years. (You'd better believe I am plenty interested in it now.) I must also candidly say that these miracles never happened when I was not interested. After I became open to God in this matter, they have been occurring more frequently as the years pass.

I want to make the point that, if we are "surprised by joy" and the word of God comes to us personally and unexpectedly, it is often a trustworthy sign that it is from the Lord. When God speaks so clearly there's no way we can miss it.

Another caution is in order here. This kind of faith is a gift from God (see 1 Cor. 12:9). It is not a gift given us to keep like a watch given for Christmas, which we can pull out and use any time we wish. It is a gift given by God in specific situations of His own choosing. Just as we do not manufacture "leadings," neither do we conjure up spiritual gifts. God gives us His presents sovereignly. I do not try to imitate your gift list, nor do you barter for mine. Though I believe we need to pray and yearn after spiritual gifts (the Bible tells us to do so in 1 Cor. 12:31), nonetheless we do not dictate these matters to the Lord.

Furthermore, God's personal word for us may not always be what we want to hear. When Paul asked God to heal him of the "thorn in the flesh," Paul accepted the answer God had for him, that God's grace was sufficient. But I daresay it was not the answer Paul would have chosen.

There are times when it seems that God's eternal Word may be yes but His personal word for us may be no. His answer to Paul certainly suggests this. But this is not because God is whimsical, undependable, or capricious. It is because He is going to keep right on being God. He has not only established His eternal truth in His Word, but He also applies it as He wills in order to assure it will not be abused.

If He is going to continue to be God, that means there will continue to be more questions than there are answers in this life. When there are no more mysteries in our walk here on earth, then God will no longer be God. And there appears to be no imminent danger of that happening!

I have described one of the wonderful ways God has of letting us know when He is saying yes. But I need to make clear that He is not limited to the personal word for us. He has other ways to work His desires in our lives, and many of them are deliberately designed to keep us humble and help us keep a proper perspective. Here is what I mean.

That same night the word of God came to me personally as I prayed with the woman in the car something else took place. Later, at the close of the service, a minister and his wife came to the altar and asked me to pray with them about a problem that they outlined. I offered prayer for the problem, and they gratefully thanked me.

The very next day at noon this minister told me of a severe throat problem he had been experiencing. After speaking, his throat would swell until it took conscious effort to force air into his lungs. His throat remained somewhat swollen continually.

"While you were praying about this other problem last night my throat was healed," he told me. "I noticed a distinct difference and this morning I went back to my doctor. He examined my throat, looked puzzled for a moment, and then said, 'Your throat is perfectly normal—you have had help from something beyond the medicine I have been prescribing!' " My friend has had no further problem with his throat.

In the healing of my minister friend it was as if God was saying to me, "I am saving you from any pride you might be tempted to allow to creep in over the healing of the woman in the car by showing you I can heal without your prayers and without giving a direct word to you. Always remember that I am the Healer, not you!"

That incident happened over two years ago. At various retreats since then I have seen the woman who had the abdominal mass. She is perfectly normal now. When we meet, we have our own little session of rejoicing and praise.

And when God showed me the lesson in the whole affair, I did some rejoicing myself. We need always to remember that God meant it when He said, ". . . I *am* the LORD that healeth thee" (Ex. 15:26 KJV). We must always remember that. There is no healing power within us without Him.

What if the personal word does not come? What if we are alone in the midnight with the beloved and the angel of death hovers perilously near and there is no word from the Lord? What then?

Can we pray on the basis of God's eternal Word? Can we lift up a promise, remind Him of it, and pray positively and firmly and expectantly with faith? Yes, we certainly can. We are invited to do so and we should. I am only saying that we have no right to claim a personal, direct word from the eternal Word when there is none. We could be sowing seeds for disappointment. In my opinion that is what happened in the case of the little child who died from swallowing the coal oil.

Does God work miracles when there is no personal word from Him? Oh yes—many, many times. The resurrection itself is proof of that. When Jesus hung quivering in His last moments and cried out of depths we can never comprehend, "My God, my God, why hast thou forsaken me?" (Matt. 27:46 KJV), there is no record of any answer from the Father. When our Savior died, He had no personal word from heaven. He died desolate and forsaken. But out of His eternal truth and His divine power God the Father acted, and from that eternal truth the power of death itself was vanquished.

Faith in the Promiser always takes precedence over faith in the promise. A lesser faith concentrates all its energies on the promises; it concentrates all its faith on faith itself. A greater faith always concentrates its best energies on the Promiser and thus walks constantly on supernatural ground.

Simply because I have been recounting cases of healing in response to God's personal word to me, I would not have you believe that healing always happens in response to the "right" word, or that if you haven't experienced some kind of healing, you are a second-class disciple.

I would not have you assume that my faith is greater than yours and that is why God acted. Such an idea is patently false and extremely harmful, for it produces loads of false guilt that people do not need to bear. People who experience the gift of faith and are honest about it will be the first to admit that there are far more people who go away from healing services with no apparent answers than there are those who experience sudden healing miracles. When God says no we must not conclude that it is always because of a lack of faith.

It is true that God is sometimes hindered in His desire to heal us because of unbelief. Jesus did no miracles in His hometown due to their unbelief. Faith sets God free to do what, by His own self-limitation, He could not do until He found belief. But faith is not the only factor involved when the desired results are not forthcoming. There are other reasons known only to God, such as the reason for the thorn in Paul's flesh. Although I do not know all God's reasons, I can still stake my life on the belief that God's eternal Word is always true, that His personal word to us in a circumstance is true, and that we must walk in the light until more comes.

One pastor tells how, in his younger days when he was touring the country and preaching in different cities with long lines of people coming for healing in his services, frustration and despair began to fill his heart. Some people were experiencing healing miracles, but by far the majority were going away disappointed.

One night after the crowd had gone home he went out and wept. It had been a night when very little had happened; yet there had been dozens of the sick and crippled in the line. "Why, Lord, why?" he cried. "I have preached Your Word; I have been as faithful as I know to be. The promises are written in Your holy Word. Why are so many going away unhealed?"

As he sat there in tears, it was as though the Holy Spirit said to him, *You do the praying, and I'll do the healing.*

Right on! That's the kind of God we see in the Scriptures. This is the God Jesus Christ reveals. I can pray positively, expectantly, and with deep faith to God the Father. I can stand on His promises and let Him deal with my prayers out of the unknowable depths of the fountain of His wisdom.

The Scriptures tell us some of the reasons God says no. We know, for example, there is nothing that blocks God from honoring our faith like a forgiven person who is an unforgiver. I have been amazed at the number of Christian people who have confessed festering resentments, particularly toward parents, which they have carried in their hearts for a lifetime and then have seen God work in a powerful way.

Then, too, we are asking for instant results. If we turn away from our prayer chambers (or from healing lines) and we haven't seen a great awe-inspiring miracle, we conclude God has said no—or that we failed in our faith.

In fact, instant results are the kind God gives the least often. In healing, for example, He sometimes leads us to natural remedies, or He does it gradually over a period of time far more often than He grants instant results. This says to me in most cases this is a *better answer* than an instant and obvious result.

We may be asking God to heal *symptoms*, and He wants to heal *causes*. Jesus did not come to deal with symptoms. His very name means "Savior from sin," and sin is a cause. Could it be that sometimes people do not experience a miracle from God because they are asking Him to deal with cosmetic problems? If your doctor is treating only your fever, for example, and not the infection, you had better find another physician.

This is why we cannot use the faith promises as mere mechanisms or formulae to force God to do what we ask. It is why other people who are saying "All you have to do is . . . " are referring to a god who seems to me to be less than God. That god is a healer of symptoms.

Here is a person who hates his neighbor with a passion. His heart is filled with bitterness and festers with deep pools of ill will. Yet in another facet of his life he is a person of great faith. He claims a promise and holds his hands which are twisted with arthritis for healing. But perhaps the arthritis is a symptom of the deeper problem. Medical journals tell us that some cases of arthritis are psychologically induced. Is God going to ignore the cause, treat the symptom, and allow the person to go away with his problem untreated? It seems highly unlikely, doesn't it?

How can you know when God is saying yes?

Springfield, Missouri, is about seventy miles down Interstate 44 from where we live. We seldom go there to visit, maybe once every year or two, simply because our schedule does not allow us to go more often. But some time ago we planned to spend the day there shopping.

As Martha and I were having breakfast that day the phone rang. The caller was a friend who said, "Arnold, do you ever go to Springfield?"

"Yes, why?" I said.

"Well, Brother Everett (a retired preacher friend) is in the hospital there, and tomorrow they are going to amputate his leg. If you happen to be down that way in a day or two . . . he's mighty blue and. . . ."

I interrupted him. "Why, we're leaving for Springfield in about thirty minutes. We'll head straight for the hospital."

I barely had time to sit down at the table to tell Martha before the phone rang again. This time it was a friend who lived in a parish on the other side of Springfield, where I had once served as pastor.

"Arnold," he said, "I don't know if you and Martha ever go to Springfield, but I just wanted you to know Jane [his wife] is down there in the hospital. She has lost the sight of one eye and is losing the other . . . and, well, I just know she would love a visit from you two."

"Man," I said. "We're on our way now!"

We got in the car and started out with hearts pounding from excitement. We knew we had had a direct, personal word from the Holy Spirit Himself.

Needless to say that was a glorious day for both of us and, we trust, for the others. There was no doubt we were to go to Springfield. God, who notes even the fall of a sparrow to the ground, saw an opportunity to bring words and prayers, comfort and healing to two of His suffering servants. And He spoke a direct word to us because He knew we would hear His voice.

There was no bright shining cloud or Damascus-road encounter. We saw no red, blue, and green disco lights whirling. God did not speak through some deep inner voice.

He used two people and prompted them to make telephone calls. It was that simple. Yet we all knew that we had heard directly from the Lord God of Hosts!

It is in this way you, too, have heard Him—many, many times. I know that you have. Just stay alert, so that you do not miss Him when He wants to speak.

How can you know when God is saying yes? Speaking of Jesus Christ, Paul says: "For all the promises of God find their Yes in him" (2 Cor. 1:20). Simply place your constant trust in Jesus Christ. Glory! What a place to find our yeses!

V

Will Faith Make Me Rich?

It is profitable to serve God, there can be no doubt about that. But He is no celestial cash box that we can open, provided we find the right combination of prayer and faith.

If your grocery money won't stretch until the end of the month, it might not always be because of inflation. Poor management and planning might be the culprits. It seems to me that most miracles happen *after* we have loved God with all our heart and mind—and still have need.

A person can sit in his living room and pray that God will drop a loaf of bread in the front yard until he starves to death. I do not believe he will get that loaf of bread no matter how much faith he has or how many promises he claims.

On the other hand, take the example of Captain Eddie Rickenbacker, who was adrift in a life raft on the Pacific Ocean with several other people for forty-five days. When they ran out of water, they prayed and a rain squall, which was about to miss them, turned and passed over the raft, filling it with fresh water. They ran out of food and were starving; a sea gull lit on Rickenbacker's head, and he was able to capture it and find nourishment. Human helplessness and desperation can set the stage for a "supernatural" miracle from God.

It is profitable to serve God, not because he is a cosmic banker or head of the New Jerusalem Welfare Agency, but because of *the law of the increasing return* (my terminology) by which He operates the universe.

It is stated in the New Testament (God's terminology) in many ways. Here are a few portions of Scripture that tell of this law.

> "Give, and it will be given to you; good measure, pressed down, shaken together, running over, will be put into your lap. For the measure you give will be the measure you get back" (Luke 6:38).

> "Truly, truly, I say to you, unless a grain of wheat falls into the earth and dies, it remains alone; but if it dies, it bears much fruit. He who loves his life loses it, and he who hates his life in this world will keep it for eternal life" (John 12:24).

> . . . whatever a man sows, that he will also reap (Gal. 6:7).

This law means the giver always receives in return more than he gave. This is true of humans and this is true in nature. Sow one grain of wheat; it gives back about sixty per stalk. Be a blessing to somebody, and you always become more blessed than they. To put it into an expression common among Christians, "You cannot outgive God."

Before we pursue this further, I must point out that this great law has a negative side as well as a positive side. Here are a few Scriptures that point this out very plainly:

. . . they sow the wind, and they shall reap the whirlwind (Hos. 8:7).

. . . Will a man rob God? Yet ye have robbed me. But ye say, Wherein have we robbed thee? In tithes and offerings. Ye are cursed with a curse: for ye have robbed me, even this whole nation (Mal. 3:8,9 KJV).

. . . and sin when it is full-grown brings forth death (James 1:15).

There are dozens of passages that state this law in many different ways, some emphasizing the positive and some the negative.

The law itself is impersonal. It never selects people to "pick on." It does not single out individuals; it operates equally for all—in perfect justice—because God has made it operate.

God never breaks His laws; He simply fulfills them. Jesus said as much. On the cross He fulfilled the law He had given. He became that grain of wheat that fell into the earth and died and, as a result, He bore the fruit of literally millions of brothers and sisters. God gave His only Son and received in return as many children "as the stars of heaven and as the sand which is on the seashore" (Gen. 22:17).

To tithe is part of this law. Whoever tithes will be blessed and will not suffer because of it. Let a person hold back his money, and he not only robs God, but the Devourer—Satan—will gobble up his finances. Whoever gives above the tithe will be blessed by the law of increasing return. The promise is:

Bring the full tithes into the storehouse, that there may be food in my house; and thereby put me to the test, says the LORD of hosts, if I will not open the windows of heaven for you and pour down for you an overflowing blessing. I will rebuke the devourer for you, so that it will not destroy the fruits of your soil; and your vine in the field shall not fail to bear, says the LORD of hosts (Mal. 3:10,11).

"Seed faith" is one popular name for this type of giving; giving that frees God to allow His law to operate in the life and circumstances of the giver.

Many years ago when I was a teacher in the public schools I saw a dramatic example of the way this principle works. The time was the very heart of the Depression, and it was also the Christmas season. Martha and I made a covenant that each of us would take a silver dollar to do something that we felt would be pleasing to God. We also covenanted not to disclose to each other what we had done.

In my class there was a little freckle-faced girl with shining black eyes and long black hair. She was a beautiful child, but her self-image was very low. She was so shy she would scarcely lift her eyes when I spoke to her. Amy came from a home that was poverty-stricken. Her clothing was made by her mother from cheap remnants and scraps.

But from time to time I thought I saw a spark of something great in Amy. I took her aside and told her of the covenant my wife and I had made. Then I said, "Amy, my dollar is going to you because I believe you are the most worthwhile and deserving young person I know."

Years passed. One night I was speaking in Lexington, Kentucky. Afterwards a lovely, well-dressed, poised, and mature woman came up to me and said, "Dr. Prater, it would be a miracle if you remembered me, but I am Amy Patterson, the girl to whom you gave the silver dollar." She told me how she had received her Ph.D. in mathematics and was a professor at a great university in that state.

We have kept in touch since then, and Amy has told me more than once how my simple gift expressing love and confidence made the difference. She said, ". . . and you can be sure that since then there have been many Christmases when I have given away silver dollars!" Increasing returns!

Jesus said, ". . . good measure, pressed down, . . . running over . . ." (Luke 6:38). You think that didn't happen to me when I met Amy again after all those years? I was so blessed every meadowlark in Kentucky was jealous! I am still blessed just thinking about it. And as I write this my heart is singing and I am whistling, "To God be the glory!"

Once, when I was speaking in a southern city, we were invited to the home of a young married couple who obviously were struggling financially. They served four of us a full and rather lavish meal. They were so happy and vivacious and joyful during the dinner party that I suspected there was a miracle story behind it all.

I was right. As we were preparing to leave, the husband took me aside and said, "Dr. Prater, I just have to tell you this. God is so faithful. We wanted to have you so badly that my wife and I agreed that, though we couldn't afford it, we'd just go ahead. We prayed that God would make a way for us."

He stopped for a moment, swallowed hard, and said, "My father died last winter. Yesterday in the mail was a letter from my mother with a check for sixty dollars enclosed. Mother said she had come across Dad's silver cigarette case, sold it for sixty dollars, and decided we should have the money because we could probably use it. Was that a miracle or not?"

"Yes," I replied, "No doubt about it. That was a miracle of God." The law of increasing return had operated. You see, that law is not only theologically true, it is practically true in everyday, Monday morning, wash-and-iron circumstances. It is " 'more blessed to give than to receive' " (Acts 20:35).

While we're on this subject of miracles, let me make a parenthetical comment. There are two types of miracles. I call them *Class A* and *Class B* miracles. Class A includes such things as resurrections, ascensions, and calming seas—the "heavy" ones. Class B miracles include God's providing money, stopping sniffles, helping you find a lost item. If your faith wavers, start trusting Him for little things, at the Class B level.

Cast your bread upon the water and you may receive a bakery in return! Give a cup of cold water in His name and you will not lose your reward.

I was explaining this law to a man once, and he said, "If I really believed that, I'd give God everything I own." Well, I could have said that was a completely illogical statement since God owned everything he had already. But I didn't. What I did say was, "This is no gimmick. It is not a formula by which you can 'con' God into performing for you. This is a law of God."

The law has both a positive and negative connotation. If one gives to God with impure motives, he or she reaps the fruit that impure motives produce. Jesus Himself indicated the kind of fruit impure motives produce.

> When you give alms, sound no trumpet before you, as
> the hypocrites do in the synagogues and in the
> streets, that they may be praised by men. Truly, I say
> to you, they have received their reward" (Matt. 6:2).

He did not say they have *no* reward. The law of the
increase worked even for the hypocrites. They had the
reward that impure-motive giving produces: a swollen ego,
satisfied vanity, false flattery, and temporary glory.

A few years ago when Martha and I began the practice of
"over and above" giving, we were heartily surprised that
God is not limited to blessing the giver in kind. We gave an
amount of money as a "seed" gift and then prayed that God
would give us "eyes to see," eyes with which to recognize
the return blessing when it came. To our surprise the
blessing was not money at all, but a new dimension in our
personal relationships which proved to be a far greater
blessing to us than money could ever have been.

Here I must stop once more to emphasize that no law of
God can be formularized as a gimmick to get what we want.
That is sin and nothing less. We cannot claim the blessing
and say, "God, You said in Your Word that all we had to do
was ask and we would receive so here is fifty dollars and we
are expecting a new four hundred dollar refrigerator in
return."

We are to ask God for specific things, but I seriously
doubt if it is "good praying" to name the specific blessing
we desire as a result of our giving. Might it not be better if
we trust Him to select the blessing? Doesn't He know our
needs already? And isn't He always working for our best
interests?

Which takes the greater faith: to say, "Lord, here is X

dollars, in return I would like objects A and B"; or "Lord, here is X dollars, You know our need and desires, and we praise You for the blessing You are going to select for us. Give us eyes to see so we won't miss it."

There are those I have mentioned earlier called "name-it-and-claim-it" Christians who say you can claim new houses, cars (usually Cadillacs), boats, second homes, and anything else you please. All you have to do is lay claim to one of the faith promises, and God will do it because His Word says He will do it. Furthermore, you can "claim" with your bank statement. I know one couple who got in serious trouble through such "full-faith" teaching. They wrote a check, having no funds in the bank, claimed the promise, and trusted God to provide the money before the check cleared. Their presumption was followed by an overdraft statement and indebtedness.

I keep repeating: I am not downgrading the Bible. I am trying instead to upgrade our understanding of the majesty of God. God cannot be manipulated, formularized, or made a party to covetousness—a sin which He regarded as so serious He forbade it in one of His Ten Commandments.

Another principle operative in this law is that we should not give simply whenever we see the need. This is very difficult for many people to see. It takes some maturity. Most of us were taught that we should give *only* where we see the need. But it may be, for example, that the one I perceive to be in need may be under divine discipline. To bankroll the person could even be to support his sin and cause me to be quenching the Holy Spirit. If I hop from need to need I am in danger of growing a Savior-complex in my giving practices.

God Himself does not always give on the sole basis of

need. Now that is a hard statement to accept. If He did, there would be no starving people in the world. God gives out of His complete knowledge of the situation.

This says to me, then, that we are to give *as we are directed by the Holy Spirit*, not merely as we perceive needs. Sometimes He may ask us to give where we see no need. It is always more important to *obey* Him than to see and understand. Martha and I are at the present time giving to two ministries where there is no great need apparent. We simply are obeying what we perceive to be His leading. He does supply our need. That is His promise:

> And my God will supply every need of yours according to his riches in glory in Christ Jesus (Phil. 4:19).

The problem in this entire matter is that some have assumed that this promise includes what we *want*. But wants and needs are two vastly different things. Any mother who has ever taken her little child to the supermarket knows that!

There is a school of thought that presumes *we* can determine what we need. But, under this presumption, needs often turn out to be wants and the wants turn out to be covetousness. The promise is stretched to mean we may obtain anything we want through the exercise of faith. In the process God is turned into a benevolent banker with an endless supply of cash, and we are the customers with an endless supply of blank checks.

What to do? I say pray for what the Father, Son, and Holy Spirit tell us are our *needs*. Stand squarely upon the promise and "let your requests be made known" (Phil. 4:6). Always allow God to be the final judge of what our true needs are. He is the only one who has all knowledge of the consequences of His answers.

To do otherwise is to give in to the same temptation into which Eve was drawn. The enemy drew her into conversation concerning the fruit in the Garden. He said to her, ". . .'You will not die. For God knows that when you eat of it your eyes will be opened, and you will be like God, knowing good and evil' " (Gen. 3:4,5).

Anyone can see Satan was actually saying, "If you take my suggestion and eat the fruit, *you will know as much as God!*" That was a lie. And it is not two inches from the temptation in the Garden to the teaching that "if we have enough faith we can have what we want." Or that we will have the power to heal everyone, and we ourselves will never become ill. Or that we will be rich!

Can you see how deceptive it is to believe the Tempter who says, "All of this will be yours, for you will know as much as God. You will know the best possible answer for your circumstances, and all material things will be under your control"? (Provided, of course, you have enough faith!)

Will God make me rich? He might. He certainly prospers us as a result of our faith; He honors His law of the increase. Whether or not you become extremely wealthy as a result of your faith in His promises rests ultimately in His perfect will and complete knowledge of you and your situation. That is because God is always going to be God. He is never going to give up His Lordship because of His supposed vulnerability to our faith. If He did, his last name would not be Omega!

David Ripley is a former law officer whose wife suffers from a lingering disease that keeps her in and out of hospitals. David found Christ in the midst of all their problems. He is now engaged in a full-time ministry in South America for a few months each year, and then he comes back to the States to preach and teach.

If faith is measurable, David Ripley has it by the truck-load, the shipload, the trainload—enough to fill the Grand Canyon to the brim. If I have ever known anyone completely yielded to the lordship of Christ, that one is David Ripley.

In his testimony he tells, "For the five years since I was born again, we have prayed, believed, and asked. I do not know why, but my wife still has the disease, and I am ten thousand dollars in debt. I do not know why this is, but I do not need to know. The thing I do know is that God is good and He is faithful and He is worthy of the last ounce of trust and faith that I have in my being!"

I don't know about you, but that is what I call a great faith. I would not want to be the one to go to David as one who has "found the truth" and say, "If you and your wife would have faith and take God at His word, He would heal her and pay off that ten thousand dollars." That would be a statement only one who considered himself spiritually elite would make.

That would be the same as saying, "I know as much as God. I know exactly the answer He will give because I know the thing that is best for you." It would simply be an instant replay of what happened in the Garden of Eden—and we are still in trouble today because of the fallout from that incident.

There is something missing from the kind of faith system that says God is a Visa Card God and with faith we can have anything we want. Or that every child of God ought to have a second home at the lake with a speed boat and perhaps a jet plane thrown in, as well as stocks and bonds without number.

There is something wrong with that, or else Paul, a prisoner of Jesus Christ, missed the boat. He told how he was a faithful servant of the law, born into the upper level of society, with status and clout to spare and then said,

> But whatever gain I had, I counted as loss for the sake of Christ. Indeed I count everything as loss because of the surpassing worth of knowing Christ Jesus my Lord. For his sake I have suffered the loss of all things, and count them as refuse, in order that I may gain Christ and be found in him . . . (Phil. 3:7–9).

Dear friend, what I am really pleading for is *balance*. Certainly God is a provider. We can take Him in as the Senior Partner in our businesses and many, many Christians are prospering because they do. God is interested in our material wants and needs, and we have every right to involve Him in every facet of life. Jesus Christ is Lord of all!

But let us not presume to have found a system in His precious Word whereby we can make Him our mindless lackey. To do so is to major in minors (or errors); it is also illusion because God is not about to give in to our every desire. If He did, he would be unloving and less than God.

It is *balance* to live every day by the Word of God, to revel in it, to immerse ourselves in it, to praise Him for the insights which constantly come from it. When we come to mysteries for which we are not ready, we need to trust Him always.

Balance means the one thing we will major in is Jesus Christ. The only thing we will be closeminded about is His blessed atonement, death and resurrection, the forgiveness of our sins, and the promise of abundant life in the here and eternal life in the hereafter.

Then shall we expect no reward at all? I tell you frankly I used to be one who would piously murmur, "I do not give expecting something in return. I give only because I love the Lord."

Well, talk about healing! The Holy Spirit healed me of that kind of talk. Faith is not faith if it doesn't *expect* something! Faith is not some ethereal kind of thing that hopes in nothing, believes in nothing, endures nothing. Faith is expectation and assurance in God.

I was taught as a child I should not do anything good in hope of a reward. I do not believe that emphasizes God's nature so much as it does ours. Jesus talked about rewards and defined them. He said we ought to lay up for ourselves treasures in heaven, rewards to be received later on.

The Bible plainly teaches rewards in heaven. When Paul says, "For we must all appear before the judgment seat of Christ . . ." (2 Cor. 5:10), it sends a chill down the back of those who don't know their Scriptures. The Greek word here is *bema*, a word the Greeks used for the judge's seat which the winners in the Olympic games approached to receive their prizes and laurels. The prospect of that is not chilling, it is thrilling.

In fact, God's salvation and the resulting eternal life are His free gifts to us. But all else in heaven seems to be based on a reward system of some kind or another. In any event, rewards are the starting point of life in the hereafter.

The Scriptures talk about rewards here in this life as well. Sow love and harmony in the home, and reap the happiness of children who sow love and harmony. Sow proper diet and exercise, and reap a wholesome body. Sow trust in God, and reap peace of mind and serenity. Sow a smile, and reap several in return. Sow a sacrifice for someone and reap a few for yourself. The "abundant life" that Christ came to give us in the here and now is brimful and running over with rewards.

Think of your life before you met Jesus Christ and think of it now. If you will, I will not need to pursue this thought further. Following Him doesn't make life easy, but it insures reward after reward after reward for endurance and faithfulness.

Will my faith make me rich? It certainly will. It will make you the richest person on your block: rich in love, faith, and maturity. The old song has it right, "The longer I serve him the sweeter it grows." Glory! It's the truth.

You cannot outgive God. He'll outdo you every time. A little boy sat in church with his mother. As the offering plate was passed he reached down into his pocket among his marbles, his knife, and other assorted miscellanea, fished out a nickel, and dropped it into the plate. Then he leaned over and whispered, "Mom, I just bought a nickel's worth of God!"

Right on, little fellow. You did. What an investment! It is God's very nature to give. As the hymn has it:

> My father is rich in houses and lands
> He holdeth the wealth of the world in his hands.

Give and it shall be given unto you. But do it as a servant, not a speculator.

VI

Let's Talk About Faith and the Will of God

The other day I went into a store to buy a pair of socks. I wear size 10, but as I searched through the sock displays I discovered a marvel of technology. They have just about stopped making socks in sizes. I mean, one pair will stretch to fit feet of differing sizes. I bought a pair marked, "Fits sizes 10 through 13." I took them home and tried them. Sure enough, they fit perfectly.

Some people are using the term "the will of God" like stretch socks. They stretch it to make it fit any situation. This works for socks, but not for sanctity—or sanity! The result is widespread confusion.

On television a young man who lost his legs in Vietnam said, "I don't know why it was God's will to take my legs from me." If you translate that it comes out, "It was pretty shabby of Him to do it and I'm angry with Him."

A priest stood outside a burning orphanage in a northern state. There were children trapped inside. The wire services quoted him as shaking his head sadly and murmuring, "It is the will of God."

A woman sat in the waiting room while her husband was undergoing radical surgery. After a long while the surgeon came out with the sad news that the patient had suffered cardiac arrest and, despite their efforts, had died on the

85

operating table. The wife sobbed as her daughter held her in her arms, "It was the will of God to take him home."

What is this? If the operation had been successful would the surgeons have succeeded in *outsmarting* God? Or were they *battling* God in that operating room?

Leslie Weatherhead in his marvelous little book *The Will of God*[5] says the term *God's will* is too big to describe all conditions and everything that happens. He breaks it down into three aspects—God's intentional, circumstantial, and ultimate will.

I believe that is a valid procedure and here's why. We have known for a long time that the highest truths must always be stated in seeming contradictions.

Jesus spoke of the "Kingdom of God" as having "already come," "now is," and is "yet to come."

Salvation in its truest sense means, "I have been saved," "I am being saved," and "I shall be saved."

If we are going to make any sense out of the term *the will of God* and its relationship to faith and His promises, we shall have to follow the same procedure. I would like to break the term down into three parts: God's *desirous* will, His *conditional* will, and His *perfect* will.

1. God has a desirous will.

If John was right and "God is love" (1 John 4:16), then we know that God only desires that which is good as far as we are concerned. Therefore we can never say that, if we run off the road and our auto turns over three times, it was what God desired to happen to us. If your baby is born with a cleft palate, it is not what God desired. If cancer invades your body and you prayed in faith and were not physically restored, you cannot say it is God's will, for He never desired that you have cancer in the first place.

Jesus made it very plain that God not only is like a good father but that He is better than a good earthly father—infinitely greater—and He will outdo our earthly fathers every time.

> "If you then, who are evil, know how to give good gifts to your children, *how much more* will your Father who is in heaven give good things to those who ask him!" (Matt. 7:11, italics mine).

If you do not believe that God is a good God and He desires only the very best for His children, you and I are on different wavelengths. Not only that, He actively works together in all things to make it come out for the best (see Rom. 8:28). When anything evil comes upon you, you can never say it is God's will in the sense that it is what He desires. Not if you are talking about God the Father revealed by Jesus Christ the Son in the New Testament.

2. God has a conditional will.

But isn't God less than God if things happen to us that He didn't desire to happen? Couldn't He have prevented them? Yes, He could have.

The truth is, He permitted them because of limitations He placed upon Himself. In order to grant us free choice, He had to grant us free movement in a world where, because of human sin, there is accident, disease, calamity, and heartbreak. It was the only way He could woo us and win us, so that we might become His children not out of fear and intimidation, but of our own free choice.

He could have placed us in a world where none of these things happen, but He was too wise for that. You could take your child out to a house in the desert and lock him in a room that is antiseptically perfect, have it heated and cooled, send his food in uncontaminated packages, and never let him have contact with the outside world. Then your child would grow up free of disease, accident, and conceivably free of all evil contacts. But I am sorry to tell you your child would be a monstrosity.

God loved us enough to place us in a world like this. Since evil has a free hand in order that we might have free choice, these things happen. God permits them, but not because it is what He would really desire.

But they happen. And then, in that situation, He has a will for us. He is working "in all things for good" for those that love Him. If we find and follow His will for us as we understand it in the situation, He will bring us through it in complete victory with great good to us and glory to Himself. Furthermore, nothing of everlasting value will be lost to us.

3. God has a perfect will.

God's perfect will for us is what He *desired* for us in the beginning. This means that His original plan for our lives will not be defeated by sin or in any evil situation. Instead, He will use even that evil situation as a vehicle to bring us to the point He desired all along. His perfect will can never be defeated unless we finally say no to His offer of salvation.

But what is His final plan for Christians? We are told in Romans 8:29:

> For those whom he foreknew he also predestined to be conformed to the image of his Son, in order that he might be the first-born among many brethren.

That verse tells the "why" of Romans 8:28.

If you leave any kind of predestinarian slant about that to the theologians, it means His perfect will for us is that sometime out in eternity He plans to complete us so that we will be full-grown brothers of Jesus Christ.

The marvel of God is that nothing that happens to us can separate us from His love and that ". . . in all these things we are more than conquerors . . . " (Rom. 8:37). One day His plan will be complete in us.

4. *What about faith in all of this?*

Faith is like a chariot in which God rides through our situations to bring His perfect will to pass. It is not a ring we put through God's nostrils so that we might lead Him about. He still navigates the chariot!

Faith is that which rises up within us after we have committed ourselves to the promises of God and placed our trust in the Promiser. Faith is what we do after we receive the leading of God. And if we are unsure of His will, we trust Him anyway!

Faith is a belief that, as God's children, we are special and unique, and that when each of us is fully grown in eternity Jesus Christ will not have another brother or sister in all of heaven exactly like us.

Faith tries with its best mind to find the will of God, but

it always trusts in the perfect will of God. It never asks God to violate His nature and, in return, He does not ask us to violate ours.

Here's what I mean. Martha has a very sweet voice—not a solo voice, but very true to pitch. Suppose Martha should say, "I am determined to be another Maria Callas (the great operatic singer). The Bible says, 'I can do all things through Christ which strengtheneth me' (Phil. 4:13 KJV), so I'm going to do it!"

I have to tell you if Martha took lessons from the finest operatic voice teachers in the world for forty years she would *never* be able to sing like Maria Callas. Why not? Couldn't she just have full faith and see it happen? If nothing is impossible with God, doesn't this approach of not asking Him to make her an opera star diminish Him? No. It makes Him bigger. He is not going to violate His own nature. He is not going to give Martha a new set of genetic equipment. Instead, He is going to *take what He gave her* and, together with Martha's faith, He is going to allow her to grow into what He intended she should become. He is going to do this in spite of her faults of heredity, her mistakes, or anything that happens to her.

He is not going to change His mind and make her another Maria Callas simply because she has faith and is quoting a text to Him. I say that makes Him *some kind* of a God. He doesn't want us to become someone other than who He meant us to be, for what He has in mind for each of us is to be someone special!

If God always has a conditional will for us, that means He will, out of His perfect wisdom and knowledge of the perfect goal He has in mind for us, give us the best possible answer to the faith we hold up to Him in that situation.

There arose a situation in Paul's life, presumably a physical condition, at any rate "a thorn . . . in the flesh" (2 Cor. 12:7). Paul asked God to remove it, but in that situation God answered that His grace would see Paul through. Another time one of Paul's companions, Epaphroditus, became ill and was near death, but he was healed after Paul evidently prayed for him (see Phil. 2:25–27). Another of his companions for whom he also presumably prayed, Trophimus, remained so ill he had to be ". . . left . . . at Miletus" (2 Tim. 4:20).

Here are three distinctively different answers to Paul's prayers. Did God have three different "wills" for him? Of course not! Whoever heard of the "wills" of God? No, He did have a conditional will for each, a will out of which His ultimate purpose would not be defeated but would indeed gain glory.

That's what happened at Calvary. When you can walk up to the worst situation that can happen to you, a cross, and turn it into the best thing that ever happened for mankind, that is the kind of miracle that springs only out of the power of our loving Father.

Dear friend, if you have cried out in the midnight of your situation and if despair has a stranglehold on your understanding, stand on who God is and on His promises. Believe that He will act in the highest and best possible way in your behalf and praise Him all the while. You will be "surprised by joy" and your miracle will be seen and felt and examined by you and others in awe and wonder. But sometimes your miracle will not be seen. You will know it is there only by faith, but it will be there! Then you can be absolutely certain about one thing.

Your faith pleases God.

VII

Questions You Always Wanted to Ask About Faith and Healing

The next time you hear a bird singing, remember it is not singing because it has answers. It is singing because it has a song!

I do not have the answers to all of your questions—or mine. I do have a song of praise and trust in my heart. That's what matters most. For the song is always more important than the answers. And if you don't have a song in your heart, the answers would only raise more questions!

We are instructed specifically to love God with our minds as well as our hearts. That instruction is given early in the Bible (see Deut. 6:5) and, as a reminder, Jesus repeated it to us again (see Matt. 22:37).

You do not stop thinking when you become a Christian. I believe many people shun Christianity because they have never really started thinking. We are to love God with all our hearts and minds, always remembering that we *find* God with our hearts and minds. We do not separate the two.

We have a song in our hearts because we have found God, and now we are trying to learn more of Him and His ways, having faith that the Holy Spirit will lead us to truth. That is His promise.

Let me repeat. I do not have all the answers to all your

questions. What I have are points of view that have been helpful to me. I have learned that, if I share things that have helped me, they usually help someone else.

The questions that are to follow are those most often asked me throughout the country in conferences and seminars and in private conversation in airport waiting rooms, motels, restaurants, and other places. Chances are you have been asking some of them, too.

1. *Does it show lack of faith if I ask God for the same thing tomorrow that I asked for today?*

People who ask this question usually have been told, "If you have asked God to heal, claimed the promise, and thanked Him for doing it, asking Him the second time proves you really didn't think He would answer the first prayer."

I disagree with that thoroughly. God is an up-to-the-moment God. His conditional knowledge is current. If there are circumstances that prevent or delay God from acting, or if "the right time" (in His opinion) has not come, then He will not say yes today. Yet He might be free to do so tomorrow. That is why the Bible is always saying to "wait upon the Lord" (see Ps. 25:3, 37:9, 62:5, Is. 40:31, Gal. 5:5).

In the matter of healing, since it is always God's desirous will to heal and since conditions in this world change every hour, we legitimately can ask God again and again for the same thing. Don't try to analyze Him or His will; just trust Him.

In the parable of the insistent widow and the judge (see

Luke 18:2–7) Jesus seems to be instructing us to ask again and again.

When I was a little boy, we frequently went to Grandma's house. It was the most exciting thing that ever happened to me as a child. It was pure heaven to "go to Grandma's." When the great day came, I would ask my father over and over, "Is it time yet? Is it time?"

He would answer, "Not yet, son," or "Be patient, son." In my childish impatience I thought we'd never be ready to go to Grandma's. Eventually the time to depart always arrived.

If it shows lack of faith to ask God again and again for certain things, why do we pray daily for our children? Martha and I pray every day that God will bless and sustain our children and their families through that day. Is that wrong? I do not think so, nor do I think it shows lack of faith. In fact, it's wrong not to!

We need to keep current in our praying, otherwise we will become like Benjamin Franklin. He told how, when he was a small boy, he used to fidget while his father was offering the table grace, for his father was an inordinately long pray-er. When they were butchering hogs in the fall for their winter's supply of meat, he asked his father if they could not bless all the meat at once so they wouldn't have to spend all that time praying at the table.

When God puts us on "hold" for reasons of His own, which He has not disclosed to us, it shows no lack of faith to repeat our petitions for the same thing daily, or even hourly, if that is what our hearts are telling us. God is neither hindered nor irritated by humble persistence.

2. Is God displeased by my lack of faith?

Remember that I said what you believe about faith tells me the kind of God in whom you believe? The word *displeased* has come to mean a reaction that contains a certain degree of petulance. I do not believe God frowns, shakes His finger, or clucks at us when we lack faith. He is not angry or pouty when we fail to trust Him, for that would indicate that He had ego problems. The God in whom I believe doesn't have an ego that has to be rein-forced constantly—and am I ever glad of that! I am glad, for I know the sometimes insatiable appetite of my own ego. How about you and yours?

But Hebrews 11:6 tells us that ". . . without faith it is impossible to please him. . . ." The entire chapter is then taken up by a review of people such as Noah, Abraham, and Moses who pleased God by obeying Him in faith.

God is pleased when He is set free to do good things for His children, because He is like a good father. It pleases me, as a father, when I am able to do something nice for my children. If I wanted to do something for them and they said, "We know more about your business than you and we do not believe you can afford to do that for us"—do you think that would please me? Not exactly!

I am sure God is sorrowful that sometimes our lack of faith blocks Him. It is comforting to me to know that He would never say what some immature earthly fathers have said: "Very well, then, if you don't want my help, forget it!"

Don't put yourself down. You probably have far more faith than you think. Remember, Jesus said it just takes a *small* amount. Besides, God is able to do much more than what we expect, in spite of our lack of faith. I praise Him right now for that! Haven't you found this to be true?

3. If I am not healed, does it mean a lack of faith on my part?

Lack of healing might mean lack of faith *sometimes*, but not always. I would go so far as to say that is very rarely the case. I have made it clear that some people are saying God answers prayer *only* on the basis of our faith. I have been saying I do not believe the Bible shows us this kind of a God.

Once more, let me remind you that Jesus healed the servant of the centurion from Capernaum and said, " '. . . not even in Israel have I found such faith' " (Matt. 8:10). He also said if we had faith the size of a grain of mustard seed we could move mountains (see Matt. 17:20). On another occasion He brought back to life the son of a widow from Nain (see Luke 7:11–16) and never once mentioned faith, or a lack of it.

Here we have three miracles of God, one as a result of huge faith, a second as a result of very little faith, and one not even indicating whether there was any faith at all. How, then, can we say that God only performs miracles according to the amount of faith one has? He has not given us that option.

Let's go again to Paul. Paul was a short, hook-nosed, watery-eyed sick man who could affect an entire city like Ephesus—a huge, sprawling metropolis, a crossroads for the flotsam and jetsam of the world, the home of a million people in the ancient world. It was the greatest stronghold on earth for the goddess Diana. Yet today you can walk into the coliseum there where twenty-five thousand people used to gather regularly to scream, "Great is Diana, goddess of fertility! Great is Diana, goddess of the Ephesians!" Then they would engage in orgies of sex and violence that would make the X-rated movie producers of today blush.

Paul could walk into a city like that with no radio, no TV, no advance publicity crew and stand among them and cry, "Jesus is Lord," until people from all over the entire city came to their knees and he established a beachhead there for Christ.

On Malta a poisonous viper bit him, but no harm came to him. God had said he was going to Rome, and Paul believed God. After that they brought him their sick, and the Bible says Paul laid his hands on them and they were all healed (see Acts 28:9). By faith he brought back to life a young man who had been accidentally killed (see Acts 20:9–12).

When you meet Paul in heaven, how would you like to walk up to him and say, "Paul, if only you had had more faith, your own thorn in the flesh would have been healed"? If you are planning on anything like that, count me out.

You think Paul didn't know the faith promises? He wrote many of them! He knew the "His stripes" passage in Isaiah 53 better than anyone. He spent hour after hour with Peter. He knew all about the Last Supper; he knew and quoted things Jesus said and did.

Paul asked God three times for healing with one of the greatest faiths in human history, and God denied him because He had *another answer* for him. One which, in God's wisdom, was better—the answer of the sufficiency of His grace.

Dear friend, do not whip yourself and wallow in self-condemnation if God seems to say no to you. In most every case I would seriously doubt that the quantity of your faith is insufficient. I do not know why you are not receiving the answer you would like. But if he really is saying no, I do know that the answer God has for you is better than what you are asking.

4. *What does it mean to live by faith and not feelings?*

When you wake up some Monday morning and the dirty clothes are piled high, two of your children are sick with colds and have to stay home from school, you have a headache, it is raining outside, and your husband leaves for work in a grumpy mood, it is not easy to feel like a child of the King. The truth is, you have the blahs.

How do you handle this?

First, don't lie to God about it. I did this for years. I would get out of bed in the morning feeling as if God were a thousand miles away, then come to my prayer time and faithfully tell Him how much I praised Him and thanked Him for all the blessings of life. I would say all the "right things" and, having done my duty, would go on about my business.

It was a great liberation for me when I finally discovered that I could be honest with God. He already knew my feelings anyhow, so I found I could say something like this: "Lord, You know how I feel this morning. I don't feel Your presence, and I don't really feel as if You hear my prayers. But Lord, I'm not putting my faith in my feelings, for I know how fickle and variable they are. I'm putting my faith in You and Your Word. You said You would never leave me. You said that I am Your child, and You have told me that You are greater than he that is in the world. And that is what I am trusting; Your Word is what I am putting my faith in, for I know it will not fail but will endure forever!"

I found that many times, affirming this truth aloud raised my feelings until I could begin the day singing after all. But even if I could not—never mind. I still would not trust my feelings. I would trust Him.

Perhaps using a more accurate term than *feelings* will explain this better. I do not trust my *moods*. Whoever puts his or her faith in moods is walking a tightrope which is dangerously weak in many places.

There was once a little boy in our church whom everybody loved. His name was Douglas, but everybody called him "Dougie." He was six years old when he contracted a case of measles. His illness was complicated in a few days by the far more serious disease of encephalitis. His condition rapidly deteriorated. Word spread around our community that Dougie was dying. His fever soared to dangerously high levels.

The next few days I thought the Holy Spirit was pressing me to conduct a prayer service for Dougie's healing. I hesitated because my mood was not particularly "spiritual" at that time.

Sometimes it is very difficult to hear God—much less obey him—when we are not "up" for it. But if we trust our "up-ness," the enemy comes against us hard with all sorts of suggestions such as, "You know it won't do any good," "You didn't really hear God's voice," or "It's just wishful thinking on your part." You know the feeling?

Our church was so concerned I went ahead with the announcement that Sunday night we would gather for special prayers for Dougie. About seventy-five people came, and we devoted an hour to prayer at the altar for Dougie and his healing.

The next morning news came that Dougie was better. Then the fever broke and began to subside. Soon Dougie was up and about, as bright and energetic as ever. A few days later his physician told me that, in his lifetime of practicing medicine, he had never seen a case of encephalitis where the patient's fever was as high as it was in Dougie for as many days, without some resulting brain damage. There was no doubt in any of our minds it was a miracle of God. (Maybe even a Class A!) Looking back, we should have had another service of prayer to praise and thank Him. But we have learned to do so since, in such instances.

I wish I could tell you that I am always successful in prevailing over my moods, but I must confess I have not arrived at such perfection. Still I hope that I am beginning to win more than I lose, and I hope that fact is encouraging to you if you have this problem.

Affirming God's great promises aloud is one of the best methods I have found by which to live each day by faith and not by mood levels. The unconscious mind hears better when the words are spoken.

This is also the way to face the great crises as well. Look at the biblical example of the three Hebrew men whom the king had thrown into the fiery furnace. Were they living life on the basis of their feelings or their mood levels when they made their great verbal affirmation of faith? Hardly. Their faith was the purest kind when they told the king,

> ". . . our God whom we serve is able to deliver us
> from the burning fiery furnace; and he will deliver us

101

out of your hand, O king. But if not, be it known to you, O king, that we will not serve your gods or worship the golden image which you have set up" (Dan. 3:17,18).

Wow! That is faith!

Consider Peter. You can read in the twelfth chapter of Acts how Herod had him arrested, promised to deliver him of the weight of his head the next day, and had him bound between two big burly soldiers. Yet that night we are told Peter was *sleeping*.

How could he do that? He couldn't have possibly foreknown the angel was coming to deliver him. If I had been told it was my last night on earth and I was chained to two soldiers, I doubt seriously I would be sleeping soundly. Would you?

Peter could sleep peacefully because in his heart the promise of Jesus was resting securely. He was still a young, strong man full of all the dynamic vitality of life, and the Lord Jesus had promised that he would not die until he was an old man (see John 21:18). In complete trust, Peter went to sleep.

The situation was impossible, but in Peter's mind that was God's problem, not his. He would let God handle it, and sure enough, as always, He did. Walking by faith is not easy, but it is a "through street." Trying to live and cope by listening to our feelings and mood levels, on the other hand, is a dead end.

5. *If I claim a promise for healing should I believe it has been done and ignore any further symptoms?*

First of all, a symptom should never be regarded as a "feeling." A symptom is rather an indication of a physical condition.

An acquaintance who dearly loves the Lord decided that faith was all she needed. She was a diabetic with a daily need for injections of insulin. She claimed one of the faith promises and stopped taking the injections. It was not very long until insulin shock occurred, and she had a close brush with death.

Surely by now most of us have matured enough to see that faith and medicine are not enemies; the doctors in this land are not at war with God. Else, what do you do with Dr. Luke who authored one-fourth of the New Testament? When people teach that "*all* one needs is faith," it must be said again and again: All healing is from God. You cannot divorce the sacred from the secular or the miraculous from the medical. God made both.

The great discoveries that alleviate human suffering and pain are *gifts* from God—things such as ether, insulin, X-rays, penicillin. Did Satan work through the minds of men to give doctors these tools with which to combat the will of God? That is the logical conclusion of the heal-me-on-demand system.

To refuse to give in to mood levels is one thing, but to ignore a temperature of 104° is quite another—especially when the aspirin that might bring the temperature down is available in the medicine chest.

I have stated that I am pleading for a balanced outlook and an end to foolhardy radicalism. Therefore I must tell you there are exceptions to what I have just said. Two years ago I had a preaching engagement in a church in a midwestern state and, during the service, the pastor called for testimonies. A young man of fifteen stood up and said he was a victim of cystic fibrosis. He was pale and thin; his voice was high and strained.

He told how two of his brothers had died of the same disease but, one night recently, God had healed him and had given him the positive assurance that he was healed.

He stood before the people and proclaimed, "God spoke to me and told me He had healed me and I am praising Him tonight that 'with His stripes' I have been healed."

Moreover, he told how on the basis of God's assurance he had stopped all medical treatment and had no intention of resuming it. To be honest with you, my faith was not very strong. I must admit I was horrified, as was most of the congregation.

This very morning I thought again of this case and wondered about its outcome. So I have just called the church long distance. The pastor happened to be gone, so I described the case to the church secretary. I asked if she recalled the incident.

She replied, "I certainly do. You're speaking about my nephew!" (Some of us quit believing in coincidences long ago!) "He never went back to the doctor for treatment for that disease. For a while, his parents almost went out of their minds. But he is seventeen now and just doing great. Remember how pale he was? Well, his cheeks are rosy and he is the very picture of radiant health."

And we praised God together.

I have said it before, and I am sticking to my guns. If you have a personal word from God, you will *know* it. Usually, you will have witnesses as well. To obey the Lord then will become the most important thing in life, and it will not be that difficult, for you will *know* that you *know*! Whoever has had a personal promise from God will have no problem with that statement; whoever has not, might. But don't make a welfare program out of a gracious gift. Don't put the promise of God on "automatic pilot" and force Him to keep it up in the same manner again and again. That, my friend, is not faith. It's presumption.

The full-faith movement is proclaiming, "Don't believe what you see, just believe what God promised." The results of this can be tragic. Again, we are faced with a half-truth designed to meet our request with the result we want and rob God of His options. Certainly many things in life are not what they *seem* to be. Many times the truth is disguised, so that the eyes will lead us to illusion. Mood levels, for instance, for the Christian are not trustworthy barometers of the conditional truth.

But if I suffer myocardial infarction of the heart, pray and claim a promise, and electrocardiograms still show gradual degeneration of my heart muscle, and if I refuse Inderal, digitalis, oxygen, or other remedies prescribed by the specialists, that is not faith. It is naiveté. It is not loving God with the mind and is likely to frustrate His will for me.

It is true that one can read testimonies of people who have been involved in terrible accidents and were brought miraculously back to health in a few days. He has done this very thing for me or through me. Therefore, I do not doubt God's power to do this.

But not to take into account the hundreds of different maturity levels of the multitudes, to prescribe "all you need is faith so ignore your symptoms" as the answer for every calamity and catastrophe, is faith worship and danger of the first order.

In addition, to deny the reality of the existence of pain and disease is basically a denial of the reality of the existence of evil. That is not biblical Christianity at all, but the basic tenet of the cult of Christian Science.

6. *If I confess it, will I possess it?*

In my opinion, in the "confess-it-possess-it" teaching we are faced with partial truth that people have seized and attempted to make into the whole truth. This is the syndrome of teen-agers who tend to discover a bit of truth and expound it as truth in its entirety.

In this case a strong argument is made on the basis of the importance of spoken words, using various biblical illustrations. Here is how the theory works: God spoke the world into existence. Then "in the fullness of time," God spoke and His Word became flesh in Jesus Christ. Then, Jesus himself said, " '. . . out of the abundance of the heart the mouth speaks' " (Matt. 12:34). Therefore, what we really *believe* and what we really *are* is eventually revealed by what we *say*.

The argument up to this point, of course, is true.

That so many of God's children are living in fear, anxiety, and defeat utterly appalls me. They miss the abundant life because they talk defeat, they talk sickness, they talk worry, they talk stress until negativism bores a hole in the cup of life and all of the halleluias are drained out. It is utterly pitiful to see disciples of Jesus Christ the victims of their own negative life-styles and habitual thought patterns.

It is bad enough that such persons miss the joy of following Jesus. What is worse is that, by constant verbalization, they unknowingly transmit these fears and negativisms into the lives of their children. This, of course, damages them and makes life a thing to be endured rather than enjoyed. When Jesus said, "'. . . my peace I give to you; not as the world gives do I give to you. Let not your hearts be troubled, neither let them be afraid'" (John 14:27), He was promising a life of victory over the world and anything its tribulations can bring. His negative children cheat themselves out of all this.

Negativism blocks God as surely as does unbelief. In a sense, it is unbelief. Martha and I have had to learn this in our own lives. What a fantastic difference it made! I have told about it in another book[6] so I won't go into detail here. I will only say we have really begun to live life on a new dimension.

Jesus never once said, "I can't, I'm afraid," or "What if?" He never spoke those words with His lips because they did not reside in His heart. It is true that the habitual positive confession of faith helps bring about the reality of bravery, confidence, joy, sensitivity to others, growing love, personal power, patience, and many, many other fruits of discipleship. I bear witness of it in my own life. I believe those who know us will tell you Martha and I are joyful persons; we do not live on cloud nine or in some kind of never-never land of unreality, but we are joyful disciples of Jesus Christ. Constant, joyful, positive confession and daily affirmation of faith have helped allow the Holy Spirit to bring this about.

But we have not discovered a "magic formula." Christian, beware and reject as false the teaching that you can possess anything you want. I am reading advertisements now of "confession" publications that promise instant prosperity, riches, job success, cars, houses—you name it. All you have to do is confess it with faith and God will see to it that you get it. Once more, we have the attempt to magnify a partial truth into the whole truth.

Only recently on television I heard a man tell how he was going from church conference to church conference telling local congregations they owed their pastors fine homes. He was quoting this Scripture:

> "And everyone who has left *houses* or brothers or sisters or father or mother or children or lands, for my name's sake, will receive a hundredfold, and inherit eternal life" (Matt. 19:29, italics mine).

Pastors have done this, so he concluded their churches owed them fine homes.

He said that in one meeting there were three lay-persons who misunderstood and thought he was speaking to them. They went out and, as an exercise in seed faith, they gave five hundred dollars to the Lord's work and confessed a new house for themselves.

The speaker heard about it later and was concerned. He called the local pastor who laughed and said, "Oh, you needn't worry about it. All three have new houses now!" Nothing to it! Just give and claim! I must confess I doubt if all the facts were told in that story.

That brings us back to the age-old attempt to box God into a corner with a formula whereby He must surrender all His options and give in to our desires. This, of course, leads to outright covetousness and, ultimately, to the sin of Adam and Eve in the Garden—the coveting of the creation itself. I am not putting down seed faith properly exercised. I have already stated my faith in that area.

Under this "full-faith" thinking, the promise is held out that we can really operate in our own little worlds on the basis of our own desires and knowledge. In effect it says to God, "I would make a better God than You!" And if that is not blasphemy, it is a first cousin to it.

I can say with absolute assurance that you can confess for yourself a desire of your own choosing until you are blue in the face, but if what you are confessing is outside of God's conditional will for you, it will never be yours.

On the positive side, verbalized faith is one of the keys that frees the Holy Spirit from His own self-limitation, and you can live life abundantly. It does not happen overnight, but when it becomes a life-style and a habitual thought pattern for you, living for Christ takes on a new dimension.

Once I read a list that a man composed and called his "Never Again" list. He named the things that he "never again" would confess. Why don't you make such a list for yourself, type it out, and put it on the refrigerator door? Include promises like, NEVER AGAIN will I say, "I can't, I'm afraid, or what if?" and NEVER AGAIN will I talk sickness, defeat, failure, weakness, or inferiority. Or NEVER AGAIN will I transmit by my words, fear, hatred, resentment, prejudice, envy, covetousness, or contempt for another person.

If I confess it, will I possess it? In God's good time you will possess what He wants you to have, for His Word says, " 'Fear not, little flock, for it is your Father's good pleasure to give you the kingdom' " (Luke 12:32).

And what is the kingdom? It is every virtue, hope, dream, and desire that is incarnate in Jesus Christ.

7. Am I to thank God for my answer before I receive it?

Recently one of the faith teachers said, "If you ask God for something you want and He hasn't given it to you yet, if you have the right kind of faith you ought to stop complaining and start praising Him that it is on the way."

Partial truth again, presented as final truth. Inherent in this statement is the now familiar concept that we can have anything we want provided we have sufficient faith. Would it not be much better to teach that we are to praise God for His answer before we receive it? This leaves Him as the final judge. In my opinion the only time I am free to praise God for *my* answer before I receive it is when the Holy Spirit specifically speaks to my heart about the matter.

If we project the faith-can-get-you-anything formula out to its logical extreme, we end up with the conclusion that no one should ever get sick. Furthermore, no one would ever choose to die physically because people would be so healthy they would all want to live on. We'd never die. That "logic" can get to be ridiculous. Where do we stop?

Jesus said, " 'whoever lives and believes in me shall never die . . .' " (John 11:26). (I sometimes marvel that someone hasn't started a movement promising to put all funeral directors out of business!)

Obviously Jesus spoke of the death of the soul. But He didn't *say* "soul." And that is the kind of trouble we get into when we try to make an entire movement out of partial truth, or out of Scripture that is taken out of context or doesn't give up all its meaning at first reading.

When we pray we ought at once to begin to praise God for His answer. The answer might be what we have prayed for. If it isn't, it will always be the best. To believe that without reservation is the highest form of faith.

8. *Am I wrong to expect spectacular answers?*

No, you are not wrong to expect spectacular answers. Remember, you are praying with faith to the God who made sunsets, the Canadian Rockies, the Swiss Alps, and the Grand Canyon. He hung the morning stars and tacked Orion and the Pleiades in place. He put a gorgeous ring around Saturn and placed with loving precision the delicate dimples in the heart of a budding rose.

But you are wrong if you expect *only* the spectacular. If you are not willing to settle for a simple, obvious answer, there will be times when you are going to miss God's will for you by a hundred miles.

I know some fervent disciples who are farmers. One of them raises hogs. Disease got into his herd and threatened to wipe it out. A couple of his friends found out about it and came over. Together they went out to the pen where he kept the hogs; there they reminded the Lord of the power He once had exercised over a group of swine. They claimed the promise that " '. . . if two of you agree on earth about anything they ask, it will be done for them by my Father in heaven' " (Matt. 18:19). They prayed over the sick hogs, thanked God for healing them, and went home.

But God didn't come through with the spectacular. He seldom does when the answer is simple and obvious—which in this case was to call the veterinarian.

We are warned in the Bible against worshiping a god who deals only in the spectacular. The fifth chapter of Second

111

Kings tells the story of General Naaman, the leper. He was the highest ranking military officer in Syria, but he had leprosy. He heard about a prophet of a God, Elisha, who could heal leprosy. The swashbuckling Naaman, along with his horsemen and chariots, set off for the prophet's house with what would be eighty thousand dollars today and many suits of fine clothing—a spectacular present for the spectacular miracle he anticipated.

If, when Naaman arrived at Elisha's humble cottage, there had arisen a mighty, thundering storm out of which red, blue, and green flashes of lightning, like heavenly disco lights, had flashed; and if Elisha's cottage had been engulfed in an orange and green glow and the prophet, in scarlet robes trimmed in gold, had stepped forth; and if from his fingers tiny bolts of lightning had issued forth striking Naaman's rotten flesh, continuing for a moment until that flesh had turned fair and whole once more, Naaman would have been thrilled beyond words. For that's the kind of god who would have impressed him. You see, many of us have a God who is small, and that's wrong. Other people have a God who is too big. That extreme is evil as well. Naaman's god was too big to be small, and a God who grew lilies in the fields and who delighted in kittens and children simply wouldn't do for him. Only a three-dimensional, one-hundred megaton god would be acceptable.

When Elisha sent word by his apprentice that Naaman had to wash in the Jordan seven times, the general was enraged. The rivers were muddy in Syria! He would not surrender his pride to a simple act like that.

The story has a happy ending. Naaman's men finally

persuaded him to swallow his pride. When he did, God worked His will for Naaman and he was healed.

Yes, we may ask for spectacular answers to our prayers, and there are times when that is what it takes. But faith is humble and never ignores the simple and the obvious. It recognizes that God our Father is the owner of all and the author of all that is fair and lovely, good and just, gracious and merciful. He is big enough to work anything spectacular He chooses, but He is also big enough to be small and simple. That is why He chose to be born in a manger at Bethlehem instead of in the temple at Jerusalem.

9. *When God heals us, do we stay healed?*

Last December, a dear lady came to me to ask for prayer. She was terribly agitated. She told me that in June God had healed her of cancer, but now she was afraid she didn't have enough faith "to keep her healing." She said, "I'm afraid it will come back."

It was obvious that her real problem was not faith, but fear. When she said, "I'm afraid," she gave herself away. She had quenched the Holy Spirit, and she was miserable.

I told her, "I don't believe God will send the cancer back into your body because of a lack of faith. God healed you because He loves you, and He doesn't want you to be afraid now." We prayed together and the Holy Spirit reassured her from within. God's love is perfect, and perfect love casts out our fears.

There is no record in the Bible of Jesus healing a person in whom that specific disease recurred. But this does not mean that if you got lung cancer from working in the coal mines and God heals you, you are free to go back and subject yourself to the conditions that caused the disease to develop in the first place.

We live life from day to day and from situation to situation. If, out of His marvelous love and grace, you receive healing from God for a disease, your body does not stop being your body. It remains vulnerable to whatever bodies are normally subjected to in a world like this.

Faith does not surround us with some kind of gelatinous, spiritual insulation that protects us from everything bad that can happen. Faith is a great preventive, and that constant positive affirmation of the keeping power of God for His children serves our mental, physical, and spiritual well-being in marvelous ways, I have no doubt. It is not magic, however. As long as we live in this kind of a world we will have to deal with this kind of a world.

Oral Roberts is a man of great faith. In a marvelous way God healed him of tuberculosis as a young man. But that did not keep him from a near-fatal bicycle accident a few years ago. I was spectacularly healed of nephritis at the age of four but in later years had serious surgery for an aortic aneurysm.

God does not guarantee that we shall stay healed the rest of our life any more than we stay clean indefinitely after a bath.

If God heals us, that ought to strengthen our faith. It should leave us so convinced of His power that we are enabled to live above fear, anxiety, and a lurid imagination. At that point it is easy for the Holy Spirit to keep us in health and well-being.

10. Is it a lack of faith to pray "if it be Thy will"?

Praying "If it be Thy will" is not a lack of faith for me. When I pray, I try to make sure which aspect of God's will I am praying about.

Some feel it is an insult to God to utter those words in a prayer for a person who has heart disease or a malignancy. If we do, that indicates God might want that person to be afflicted.

I am sure we can all agree by now that God does not arbitrarily want anyone to be ill of disease. Still, people develop "hang-ups," and if it makes you feel guilty to say those words when praying for ill persons (including yourself), then don't use them. It's no good to invite guilt feelings if we know in advance that is how we shall feel.

But asking "If it be Thy will" is not a problem for me for two reasons. One, Jesus used those words. If you will read the Gospel accounts of His soul-struggle in Gethsemane, you will see that He used them three times. Always, He left the Father the final option.

Second, I can use "If it be Thy will" because I know the aspect of God's will to which I am referring. In respect to sickness, I am never referring to God's desirous will, for I know He doesn't want our bodies to be invaded by enemies from the kingdom of evil. I am always referring to His conditional will. I might say, "Lord, grant this healing. You know what we want. Grant it to us if, in Your infinite wisdom, it is the best possible answer under this situation. And Lord, I praise You right now for Your healing answer, for I know You are faithful to grant Your children nothing but the best!" I say again, if I thought there was the slightest danger that your faith might be weakened, I would never use that phrase in your presence.

Finally, God sees beyond our words. He hears our prayers

as they should be heard. I praise His name for that. He is not distracted by our mistaken ideas and, therefore, we can pray in serenity and confidence.

So pray on. Expect a miracle. Pray with faith and joy!

11. *Is there a connection between faith and love?*

There certainly is a connection between faith and love. Faith comes in second. Faith is not the greatest thing there is. There is something that pleases God more than faith, and that is love. That is something I have been saving to say until somewhere near the end of these pages, for I realize that these questions and views could be controversial.

Let me tell you who the mature person in Jesus Christ is. He or she is the person who can reject what you believe without rejecting *you*. It is time we Christians stopped trying to defend God. He can take care of Himself. I believe it is just as important to be loving toward other people who disagree with me as it is to be correct in my views. If I am correct in my views and unloving about it, then my doctrinal precision profits me nothing.

In a world that is sin-infested and rapidly throwing overboard all the biblical values, one that has forsaken God and is hell-bent for destruction in its oil-mad rush for domination, we ought to be praying for each other instead of fighting each other.

If I am cross ways with others in my views, instead of just trying to out-argue them I ought to be trying to out-love them. Instead of shunning them because they do not see things my way, I ought to be washing their feet. Being right biblically bothers the Enemy; loving one another frightens him beyond telling.

God is a miracle-working, faith-honoring, prayer-answering, disease-healing God. His storehouse is filled with works of might ranging from the super-colossal-spectacular down to the simple, and what misguided people call the "ordinary." Faith is not the key to unlock the answers of our heart's desire; it is the key that allows God to grant us miracles beyond our imaginings and eyes with which to see them.

His Word says, "So faith, hope, love abide, these three; but the greatest of these is love" (1 Cor. 13:13). Thus love is number one because it is never distracted by error.

Faith is number two. I suppose that is why it always has to try harder!

VIII

Three Faith Prayers to Which God Always Says Yes

Unbelief is the opposite of faith, and it is a giant. You cannot play with giants; they have to be slain!

All through these pages we have been saying that God is faithful and worthy of our trust. His answers are coined out of His love and knowledge. The answers we want may turn out to be the same as His. But when they don't, it's time to coin pure trust as our response.

We have things backwards. We are inclined to trust the status quo because the future seems so uncertain. Not so. The future is unknown but certain. The present is known but uncertain, for who knows what today will bring? We do not need to fear God's answers for today.

Two little boys were in a lodge hall where their parents had taken them for a social dinner. There was a huge eye painted on the ceiling. One boy said, "See that eye? That's God's eye—it means He is watching to see if we do wrong."

But the other little boy said, "No, that means He loves us so much He can't take His eye off us!"

Right on, little fellow.

But isn't all this talk about having faith when God says no a kind of a cop-out? Is there anything for which we can ask and always be certain we shall receive it?

Yes, there are several things and, not surprisingly, every one of them is received by faith. Let me just mention three. First, when a human being asks God for salvation through Jesus Christ, God never substitutes a better answer, for there is none. God cannot deny that request because to do so would violate the very work He accomplished at Calvary.

When a human being out of free choice comes to the Father and out of personal need cries in faith, "Lord, I receive Jesus Christ as my Savior, I ask You to come in and forgive my sins and save my soul," God does just that. This is one prayer that a person may be certain God will honor, granting exactly what the pray-er asked for. The appeal of the Cross and the offer of the free gift of salvation is capable of stirring human hearts everywhere to have faith.

One of my friends who is a missionary went seventeen miles up a river in Indonesia to a little village where the name of Christ had never been spoken. He pitched his little pup tent, and the first night the villagers gathered about the campfire while he told them the simple story of Jesus.

After he had gone to his tent and had been asleep for an hour, he was awakened by a scratching sound on the tent flap. He saw a tiny, wrinkled, old man who said, "Tell me again about that Man who died for me!"

Three times before morning my friend was awakened by this man, who was awestricken by the incredulous story of a God who loved him enough to lay down His life for him. Needless to say, out of his mustard seed of faith the man eagerly gave his heart to Christ. No arguing, no theological discussion—just simple faith. God can never say no or offer a substitute when a child of His asks for salvation through Jesus Christ.

There is a second thing we may always be certain to receive when we ask, and that is *forgiveness*.

Jesus Christ arose from the dead talking about forgiveness. Peter had denied the Lord three times. Guilt had blown off the top of his heart, and he had run away into the night. When Mary met the angel in the garden that first Easter morning, Jesus sent a message by that angel: " 'Go, tell his disciples *and Peter* . . .' " (Mark 16:7, italics mine). I believe He wanted Peter to know He had forgiven him.

Later the disciples were in a room with the doors locked for fear of the authorities. All but John had forsaken the Lord at the cross. Suddenly He came and stood among them. Quickly, before they had time to feel the flush of shame and embarrassment, He said to them, " 'Peace . . .' " (John 20:19). The basic meaning of the Greek here is, "It's all right . . . it's okay."

Christians do not need to carry loads of guilt about with them, for they have been accepted of God, through Christ, and are forgiven. In trying to dramatize the limitless scope of God's love and forgiveness, the Word of God says,

> As far as the east is from the west,
> so far does he remove our trans-
> gressions from us (Ps. 103:12).

I call that my "glory psalm," for every time I read it, I just can't help saying "Glory!" When God looks at a Christian, out of His own love and nature, He can only see the absolute righteousness of Christ.

Suppose we are taking a jet plane somewhere. Before boarding we have to pass through the scanner at the airport terminal. We start through and the thing goes "Beeeeeep." The lady asks us to go back and empty our pockets. This time we walk through, and there is no beeping. We are allowed to go aboard the plane.

In a sense there is a scanner at heaven's gate. It is a sin-scanner. We walk through it, and it is so sensitive that the tiniest sin will cause it to beep. We must be entirely clean. But we cannot cleanse ourselves from sin at this gate, and only the sinless pass through. The Bible says that "All have sinned and fall short of the glory of God" (Rom. 3:23).

But Jesus Christ comes and stands between us and the scanner. His body and blood, given at Calvary, cover and shield us so that the probing beams of judgment cannot reach us. They only reach Him and they find no sin there, so we are allowed to pass through—accepted and completely forgiven, by nothing we have done but by what He has done! (Another "Glory!" here.)

That is what the Scripture means that says,

> ". . . not that we loved God but that he loved us and sent his Son to be the expiation of our sins (1 John 4:10).

So when we ask for forgiveness, that prayer is always granted, and no other answer is ever substituted. How do we know this? We know it by faith. How do we receive this? We must receive it by faith.

There is still another thing we can know for certain God is going to give us when we ask for it and that is *eternal life*.

We do not earn it. We do not mature enough to be worthy of it. We do not finally become good enough to deserve it. It is a gift from God; a gift of the Father to His children.

> For the wages of sin is death, but the free gift of God
> is eternal life in Christ Jesus our Lord (Rom. 6:23).

Receiving eternal life through Jesus Christ is not like a tiny package that is discovered tucked away after all the others have been opened. It is the biggest gift under the tree of Christmas!

Of all the gifts God could give us, this is the biggest: a big gift from a big God. How big is He?

He is the God who fashioned this little wayside planet like a boy rolling a tiny mudball between the palms of His hands. Then He made another planet and another until He had nine of them. He threw in a sun and a moon and had a solar system. Then He set them all whirling, splashed out a galaxy called the Milky Way, sequined it with sixty million glistening stars, and then rolled out an entire universe so big we can't even think our way across it.

That wasn't enough, so He made a hundred million more universes. Then He stepped out on the balustrades of eternity and gazed across the infinite blackness and said, "Let there be light," and a hundred billion silver arrows split the darkness and there was light.

Then He made us and set us here and loved us so much that when we got hopelessly mired down in our humanity He said, "I'll give them the biggest gift of all—My Son. And that means through Him they can live forever!" Eternal life with Him is the biggest gift of all.

Barbara Brokhoff tells that Alexander the Great liked to feel his subjects could come to him about any little matter. One day a saucy little beggar gained audience with Alexander, asked him for a farm for himself, a new house for his wife, a dowry for his daughter, and an education for his son.

Alexander granted the large request. When the beggar left, the men of the court said, "Why did you let that unworthy little fellow have all that? He asked for so much."

Alexander replied, "He treated me like a king. *He asked big!*" Dear friend, when we asked Jesus Christ to come into our lives and be our Lord and Savior, we asked big! We asked for the biggest thing God has.

Furthermore, even though we were unworthy, He gave us the gift. He did not scrounge for a substitute. That is the only way anyone has ever received eternal life, and whoever has asked has always received the affirmative reply. Though we do not have all the answers, by faith we have the Big Answer. We can grow our way through the rest.

I do not know all there is to know about faith. I do not understand all there is in the precious faith promises nor, I believe, does any other human being.

I do know that the Word of God is a "lamp unto my feet" (Ps. 119:105 KJV), and my Bible is my most precious possession. It is the brilliant light that is guiding my path. But lingering in the shadows of that light are mysteries that swirl and beckon me. Eagerly I press on to greater growth and deeper understanding.

You and I do not know very much about the cosmic Father who cupped out the oceans and piled up the majestic mountains. We know practically nothing about the great I AM who lives and acts eternally beyond our understanding.

But we know the story of the Man who hung on that

rugged cross outside an ancient city and who could not be held by the tomb of Joseph of Arimathea. He lives today. Those of us who have met Him are privileged to say we know Him!

We know something else, and we know it for sure. The old Sunday school hymn was right.

Faith is the victory, faith is the victory!
O glorious victory, that overcomes the world.

Notes

1. Arnold Prater, *You Can Pray As You Ought* (Nashville: Thomas Nelson Publishers, 1977).
2. *The Upper Room*, August, 1977. Used by permission.
3. *The Daily Blessing*, April-June, 1980. Used by permission.
4. Prater, pp. 67,68.
5. Leslie Weatherhead, *The Will of God* (Nashville: Abingdon, 1976).
6. Arnold Prater, *How To Win Over Frustration* (Irvine, Calif.: Harvest House Publishers, 1980).